DATE DUE			
JAN 2 2 1988			
FEB 0 8 1988			

THE WRITINGS OF

WILL ROGERS

I - 6

SPONSORED BY

The Will Rogers Memorial Commission
and Oklahoma State University

THE WRITINGS OF WILL ROGERS

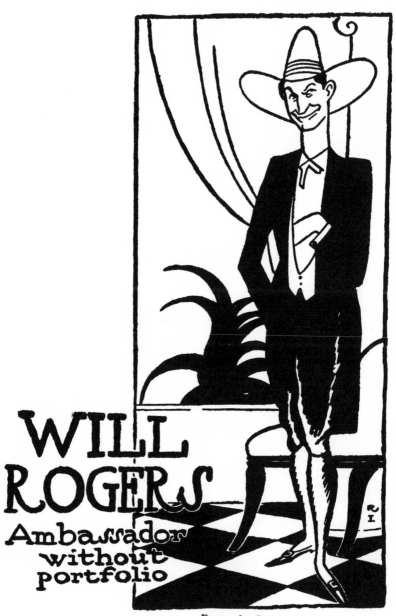

WILL ROGERS
Ambassador without portfolio

Drawn by Rea Irwin

Letters of a Self-Made Diplomat to His President

By Will Rogers

JOSEPH A. STOUT, JR., *EDITOR*

PETER C. ROLLINS, *Associate Editor*

STEVEN K. GRAGERT, *Editorial Assistant*

OKLAHOMA STATE UNIVERSITY PRESS
Stillwater, Oklahoma
1977

Note to scholars: The Boni book and the original illustrations are reproduced with permission of the Will Rogers Memorial Commission, Claremore, Oklahoma, and The Rogers Company, Beverly Hills, California. The scholarly apparatus and notes in this volume are copyrighted and the usual rules about the use of copyrighted material apply.

International Standard Book Number 0-914956-09-4

Library of Congress Catalog Number 76-47737

Printed in the United States of America

ACKNOWLEDGMENTS

Will Rogers definitely was a world traveler. He often said that all he knew was what he read in the newspapers, but this was not entirely accurate. In fact, even as a young man, Rogers had traveled around the world, and long before his entertainment career, he was more cosmopolitan than he wanted people to believe.

Letters of a Self-Made Diplomat to His President originally was published in large part in the *Saturday Evening Post* from July 10-October 2, 1926. While abroad Rogers also cabled many brief messages exclusively to the *New York Times* which featured them in boxes set apart from the rest of the news. The New York publishing firm of Albert & Charles Boni, Incorporated, collected and published the *Post* articles and many of the *Times'* "daily telegrams" with slight revisions in one volume in 1926; the book sold well at $2 a copy. Herbert Johnson provided the illustrations for the magazine and the book. Reviewers and other readers offered positive comments about the Cowboy Philosopher's contribution to diplomatic understanding.

In editing this volume of *The Writings of Will Rogers* several difficult decisions were made. As this volume originally was comprised of articles, rather than a single manuscript, and as there are no original manuscripts for the work, we have chosen the Boni publication as the basis for the text. Where the articles differ greatly from the Boni version, we have noted the changes. In addition, where an editor changed Rogers' style in some significant manner, we have shown the variations either from the *Saturday Evening Post* or the *New York Times*.

Rogers occasionally mentioned people who were virtually unknown at the time, and in these cases we have not chosen to give biographical data. Only in cases where Rogers mentioned some person, place or thing that needs explanation, have we supplied data. We have in no way attempted to interpret Rogers' text in the notes, for only information needed to place the item in question in historical perspective has been given.

This volume, the final in Series I of *The Writings of Will Rogers,* has required considerable effort on the part of a number of people. Reba Neighbors Collins, Curator of the Will Rogers Memorial, read the manuscript carefully, and offered insightful advice for the notes and introduction. Glenn D. Shirley's designs of the books continue to be a great asset to the project. Oklahoma State University President Robert B. Kamm and wife Maxine have supported the project completely and encouraged the editors to do the best possible job.

Finally, special appreciation is expressed for the continued support of the Will Rogers Memorial Commission, the Oklahoma State University Regents, administration, and advisory committee, the Oklahoma Historical Society and the Oklahoma Legislature. Earlier in the project Kerr-McGee Foundation, Phillips Petroleum Corporation, Mr. and Mrs. Robert W. Love and Mrs. T. S. Loffland provided assistance.

The Editors

CONTENTS

PREFACE

Some years ago on a transatlantic ship I encountered a retired U. S. Army colonel who had been in charge of a troop transport enroute from New York to Brest in 1917.

His ship was horribly overcrowded with more than 1,000 men stacked in tier upon tier of bunks in the hold. The U-boat menace was then at its height, and one day as the convoy approached France the destroyers got a contact.

All the soldiers were immediately ordered below. They stood, jammed in their cramped quarters, listening to the crump of depth charges and wondering at what moment a torpedo would come. Suddenly, by the unluckiest coincidence, a generator failed and the lights went out.

"In the total darkness," recalled the colonel, "the conversation ceased immediately. I could feel the tension rising like a tidal bore. I waited for the first scream of panic and the blind rush to the ladders that might kill 100 men.

"Then, out of the stygian blackness came a high-pitched Southern voice:

" 'Anybody wanna buy a watch?'

"In the explosion of laughter panic died, sanity returned, and the situation was saved."

Will Rogers would have thought of such a gag.

Oklahoma's crackerbarrel-and-potbellied-stove philosopher had a genius for easing tensions. He had the gift of making people laugh at themselves because he was endlessly laughing at himself. In the process of unstuffing shirts he made his victims love it, for there was no stuffiness in him.

There was, of course, considerable craft. He was an actor who created a role and played it fortissimo until death caught him. His affected naivete covered a shrewd mind and a calculating eye. Little that was incongruous or ridiculous escaped him. But he sugarcoated his pills with spurious illiteracy and grammatical gaffes. It was art.

I met him only once. I was in Baton Rouge as a cub reporter trying to cover an electric situation in which Huey Long had declared martial law. It was forbidden for more than six people to gather in the street. I was wide-eyed and excited, writing what I thought were dramatic paragraphs and awaiting a blood-bath that fortunately never came.

Will Rogers was calm and cheerful. His one-paragraph commentaries on the Kingfish were gently disrespectful and wryly funny.

While I was busy trying to pump up a menace, Rogers was deflating it. There was no question which was the wiser course.

No one need take at face-value his oft-repeated statement, "I never met a man I didn't like." That would have required an amoral mind. But he had the great human quality of searching for the best, not the worst. He measured length, not shortness. And thus, when he poked fun, even his victims were ready to buy.

Will Rogers is dead. We are far into the era of sick humor. We are intrigued with the put-down. We applaud the bald insult. And as our laughter has grown more vicious our inclination has grown to go for each other's throats.

Will Rogers would have had none of this. He would have un-stuffed us. Even as he had us laughing at the shortcomings of our enemies he would have had us contemplating our own. Out of this flows balance, proportion and the milk of human kindness.

The world needs a new Will.

Jenkin Lloyd Jones
Editor, The Tulsa Tribune

INTRODUCTION

Will Rogers wrote millions of words between 1919 and 1935, and in the process he entertained the American public with his "folksy" demeanor and perceptive remarks about all facets of American life. With insightful comments Rogers explained to the average citizen many of the esoteric aspects of government, including foreign relations.

The cowboy philosopher knew well that United States diplomacy with other nations had remained a mystery which most Americans had not even tried to understand. Rogers also knew that many misconceptions about American diplomacy existed; many of these still persist today. One pervasive myth has held that the United States refused to become involved with foreign countries, especially those in Europe, during the first three decades of the twentieth century. Will Rogers recognized that this country was not isolated, and he commented often about the participation of the United States in world affairs. Moreover, during Rogers' writing career, America was engaged almost constantly in some type of international conference. Significantly, Rogers' comments about society and foreign relations accurately and humorously reflected the diplomacy and the history of the era—a period of excitement and color.

By 1920 national prohibition finally had become law, and Woodrow Wilson was in his last few months as president. Rogers performed for Wilson in 1916 and for several years wrote and spoke about the president's problems in government. In his last year as president, Wilson failed to place the United States in the League of Nations, but this diplomatic failure was tempered when he won the Nobel peace prize of 1919. On August 20, 1920, Americans ratified the nineteenth amendment to the Constitution giving women the vote. This ratification occurred just in time for women to vote in the election of 1920; their votes helped elect Warren G. Harding. In November of the same year, the first national radio service began when station KDKA of Pittsburgh commenced broadcasting. Americans looked optimistically toward a decade of business prosperity. However, on July 28, 1923, President Harding became ill while returning from Alaska. He was rushed to San Francisco, and there died on August 2. The next day his vice president, Calvin Coolidge, allegedly a taciturn and dour politician, assumed the nation's highest office.

Just before Harding's death some of the questionable practices of his administration surfaced. And, shortly after Coolidge's ascension, congressional investigators exposed the full significance of the offenses.

Government officials had been involved in such oil scandals as the Teapot Dome affair. In this affair officials of oil companies and the government conspired to profit personally from United States government oil reserves in Wyoming. Numerous other scandals also emerged in 1923, and during the next year. Calvin Coolidge said little about the scandals; his silence, reputation for honesty and puritanical habits made him a stablizing force in a period of political chaos. He was so effective in this role that his party nominated him as its presidential candidate for the election of 1924. The Democratic party divided before and during the convention on issues such as national prohibition. One faction wanted as the party's candidate the popular Catholic governor of New York, Alfred E. Smith. Other party regulars would not accept Smith, and after more than one-hundred ballots, the party nominated an unknown, John W. Davis of West Virginia. Coolidge won easily.

While Republican prosperity continued, the United States participated in international conferences of several types. In 1926, after some arbitration, the country almost joined the Permanent Court of Justice at the Hague, but remained outside the international organization because of minor disagreements. However, in 1926 the United States did participate in a naval conference at Geneva. Unfortunately, France and Italy refused to attend this meeting and the members who met accomplished nothing.

By 1926 Will Rogers had a busy schedule. For example, he began a transcontinental speaking tour toward the end of January, and traveled constantly, even after he returned from Europe. The pace of his American tour was staggering. He remained in small cities one night; larger ones demanded two of the humorist's evenings. On the average, the forty-six-year-old Oklahoman visited a different American city every day. But the rewards for touring were as great as the labors. Rogers enjoyed prowling about the country, for travel allowed him to "feel the pulse" of the average Americans (whom he called "the regular birds") outside of the political and commercial worlds of Washington and New York. And the pay was excellent. Charles Wagner, manager of the tour, reported that Rogers and his co-stars, the DeReszke Singers, had grossed over $82,000 in receipts during their eleven weeks on the road.

There were competing demands for Rogers' valuable time after the national tour. On April 2 he received a telegram from Florenz Ziegfeld pleading for help. Ziegfeld had heard that Rogers was thinking about sailing to Europe at the close of his transcontinental lecture series. Hoping that the Oklahoma humorist instead would join the *Follies* for the coming year, Ziegfeld advised against leaving the country: "decide to postpone visit to Europe. Rotten over there now any-way." Ziegfeld was sanguine about the prospects for his show if Rogers would participate: "I could make the Twentieth Follies and probably the last the greatest of them all." On the telegram was a conspicuous blue stamp instructing the recipient that an immediate answer was expected. "Flo" got a negative response, for Will Rogers was determined to talk with the average citizen of Europe.

Will Rogers had joked and written about European affairs in 1919 in *Rogersisms: The Cowboy Philosopher on the Peace Confer-ence*, but he had not visited the continent in several years. Americans were curious about how Europe was emerging from the wreckage of war. And, they wondered about their international responsibilities in the postwar era, the war debt question, and the viability of the new League of Nations. Rogers was anxious to get a first-hand appraisal of these developments, and he had found a sponsor, the *Saturday Evening Post*.

On April 15, 1926, Will Rogers ate lunch with George Horace Lorimer, famous editor of the *Post*. The *Post* recently had carried a feature entitled "Letters of a Self-Made Merchant to his Son." Lorimer thought Rogers too could write a special feature series of articles taking a similar approach to the pressing foreign policy issues con-fronting the nation. Rogers already had shown considerable success in this regard with a series of weekly articles for newspapers. Lorimer believed unquestionably that Will Rogers was the best man to tackle this assignment. For several years Rogers had played the role of an Oklahoma cowboy thrown into the middle of modern America. The appeal of his social commentary stemmed primarily from his ability to judge modern developments by the values of traditional American life.

As a writer, Will Rogers had a literary problem to overcome. To whom would the letters of this self-made diplomat be sent? The cowboy philosopher knew that Calvin Coolidge was not quite as dour as the press often portrayed him. He decided to make the president his pen pal. An advertisement for the *Post* series conveyed the light tone of these letters— the ad pictured a slender man who was obviously President Coolidge facing away. Will Rogers was whis-pering to him sage counsel about foreign affairs: "Now listen, Mr. Coolidge. This is between you and me . . . and the rest of the nation." However, Rogers intended no disrespect toward the president from Vermont. On the contrary he actually admired Coolidge, whom he described as "a great politician. He looks further ahead than any of them." Thus, the letters rather than essays — from Rogers of Clare-more, Oklahoma, to Coolidge of Coolidge's Corner, Vermont — provided an excellent format for Rogers' observations as the self-made diplomat.

OVERVIEW OF THE TRIP

Will Rogers toured Europe and Russia with the same lively pace which had characterized his early spring transcontinental speaking tour. While he had no fixed itinerary for the trip, he planned to visit several countries and send back colorful and instructive copy. The title of the series might have been conceived in jest, but the role which Rogers played was ambassadorial in a serious sense: he was performing a special service for the nation. There had been so many variant reports that perplexed Americans looked forward to reading his witty opinions.

In the morning of May 1, the *Leviathan* left its berth in New York harbor carrying among it passengers Will Rogers and his fourteen-year-old son, Will, Jr. Six days later the modern liner docked in Southampton, England. After a week in London, father and son flew to Paris in a large new French airliner. It was a rough trip; a seasick and prone devotee of aviation experienced one of the negative effects of flight. Yet the next day the Americans entrained for Rome. When Rogers stopped en route to visit the disarmament proceedings in Geneva, negotiations almost ceased. The *Tulsa Daily World* proudly reported: "Will Rogers, American Lariat Artist and 'Wise Cracker' bobbed up in the League of Nations Disarmament Commission session in the afternoon and attracted more attention than many delegates."

Rogers later visited with dictator Benito Mussolini in Rome. The "non-interview" between the representative from Claremore and Il Duce was one of the more enthusiastic moments in the *Letters of a Self-Made Diplomat,* for Rogers perceived the early work of Mussolini as constructive and beneficial to Italy. (It should be noted that this evaluation preceded by four years the excesses of Mussolini's foreign policy, and that many persons shared Rogers' views at this time.) While in Rome the Pope gave Rogers an audience, but the Oklahoman did not comment about this visit. Later, Rogers journeyed to Spain for an interview with another dictator, Miguel Primo de Rivera. The traveling American democrat apparently enjoyed the traditionalism which he encountered in Spain.

Within two weeks Rogers was back in London preparing for a flight into Russia. Permission to observe the communist experiment in social engineering had arrived while Rogers was in Italy. The *Saturday Evening Post* was as obliging in this case as it had been about the

European tour, and for the same reason. Because there had been so many contradictory reports by commentators, the American people would take pleasure in a Rogers treatment of the subject. The series was published independently of the European travelogue under the facetious title, "There's Not a Bathing Suit in Russia and Other Bare Facts."

By mid-July Rogers again was back in London where he signed a much publicized contract with British National Pictures. The British hoped to break Hollywood's monopoly on film comedy. Also while in London Rogers conceived other ways to communicate with the British, and thereby pay expenses. Almost as soon as he stepped off the plane from Moscow, he signed a contract with Cochran's *Revue,* a British imitation of Ziegfeld's *Follies.* In addition, he appeared in a late night cabaret in a show similar to the *Midnight Frolics* which had made him so popular among New York's late night set. Finally, the Oklahoman created quite a stir when he went on the air in August "for the largest fee ever paid to a radio talker in this country" and then donated the fat check to a hospital charity.

Rogers' wife Betty, daughter Mary and younger son Jim joined the humorist in early August. Will, Jr. was sent home early to enter Culver Military Academy in Indiana.

Early in September Will and Betty Rogers were in Ireland, delighting in the Irish landscape, but again taking time to do benefits for charity. A tragic fire in Dromcolliher recently had killed and seriously injured scores of citizens. Rogers immediately volunteered to perform at a theater in Dublin, with all proceeds donated to the sufferers. He raised two thousand dollars at the door, to which he added a contribution of five hundred dollars. Will Rogers was fast transforming himself into an ambassador of good will!

After returning from Ireland, the comedian settled his family into comfortable quarters in Switzerland. He then left for a hasty last reconnaissance, to include Greenland, Scotland, Wales and Germany. On September 21 the family boarded the *Leviathan* for home.

As the *Leviathan* sailed for the United States, Will Rogers could total up a number of accomplishments: he had plumbed the motives of the intellectual and political leaders of the new Europe; his travels had allowed him the opportunity to talk with average citizens, the "regular birds" of the continent; and he now had first-hand information about foreign leaders and basic foreign policy matters. It was no longer true—as it had been during the war—that all he knew about Europe and its leaders was what he read in the papers. His horizons had enlarged, and his insights deepened; his observations in the future would be increasingly authoritative.

THIS COLLECTION OF HISTORICAL HUMAN DOCU-
MENTS IS RESPECTFULLY DEDICATED TO THREE
LADIES WHO HAVE THE KEENEST SENSE OF HUMOR
THAT IT HAS BEEN MY GOOD FORTUNE TO EN-
COUNTER. THEY APPRECIATE JOKES EVEN ON THEIR
OWN HUSBANDS:

MRS. CALVIN COOLIDGE[1]
LADY NANCY ASTOR[2]
MRS. ALICE LONGWORTH[3]

I WANT ALSO TO GRATEFULLY ACKNOWLEDGE
THANKS TO MRS. WILL ROGERS FOR THE SUGGESTION
OF THE ABOVE IDEA AND VARIOUS OTHERS.

PREFACE

All the big writers nowadays are fetching out their books in volumes, or a series of volumes rather. It's really the great American tragedy that it is being done that way. H. G. Wells[4] has a new serial running in half a dozen sections with a warning that he can write a five hundred page postscript at a moment's notice.

Theodore Dreiser[5] got his hero in so bad in one volume that it took another bigger one to get him executed. The day of the "one book man" is gone, the same as the day of the "one gun man" in the movies was limited. The advantages of double barrel over the old single barrel breech loading books is numerous. In the first place you can always say in the second volume what you forgot to say (or hadent read probably) in the first book. Or, more handy still, you can use it for denial purposes. I hope to be like a good book-keeper: when my volumes are finished my accusations and denials will balance so even that I havent really said a thing. Then there is a sales value, two or three volumes are harder to push out of the way in a bookstore than one volume is. So this little work you are fondling now is really just a preface, or foreword, and if there is any little problem confronting the reader that is not made entirely clear why don't miss about the eighth volume, it will be solved I am sure to your entire satisfaction. If not we can always add another volume, for I just bought a new typewriter ribbon. More ideas havent length-ened books—its easy working typewriters that have done it. Writing today is based on endurance not thought, and I am going to give my public the advantage of a wonderful physical constitution while it's at its peak. I know when you read this volume you will say: "I want Volume Number Two, it must be better."

WILL ROGERS

Author's Note

The author has been reluctantly willing during these trying days of April, June and July, and February, which has but twenty-eight when leap year comes and brings it twenty-nine. He has allowed the President[6] to receive all the glory and has kept himself in the background.

This is unique in Memoirs or Autobiographies. I am publishing what was done and said while all the Parties concerned in these narratives are alive. I could have waited a few years till some of the actors who stalked across the stage in this great drama of human events were dead. But I said No. These are facts, and if there is a man connected in anyway with them who dares to dispute them, let him rare up on his hind legs and proclaim it himself. I have always felt that a man can defend himself better than his remaining relatives. Then besides there was always the possibility of me passing out first.

The reader must bear in mind that these communications treat only with subjects that come within the orbit of my own activities. The President and his Cabinet have dealt with many little minor affairs that is not dealt with in these narratives at all, because I couldent see personally after everything. So naturally I just took up the more important.

These were compiled by Mr. Nicholas Murray Butler,[7] president of Columbia University, One Hundred and Fifteenth Street and Broadway, New York City. And if any blame is attached, why, kindly take it up with him. If he has seen fit to omit any little passages, or add in any, why, he has done so without advice of Consul. Now if at any time I have assumed a rather critical attitude toward some of the Actors in this Comedy of Errors, why, the chances are I have been really to lenient with them. As for the Principal Character Our President, I must frankly admit that I am a partisan of his. Any man that knows enough to say nothing always wins the admiration of those of us who feel that we can do the talking much better than he can anyway. Now, of course, now and then, he and I have differed. It takes a smart man to differ with me.

The President realized that Mr. Stearns[8] was doing everything humanely possible in a domestic way, but that the time had come for the President's influence to branch out; and that someone should be sent to Europe if He, the President's name, was to be perpetuated in two vulumes with foreign date lines. Senator Butler,[9] of course, was thought of. But with other worries[10] he wouldent even have time to say Europe.

My trip come at a time when foreign relations are at their most perilous peak; that is, when we were trying to collect money.[11] Any man[12] can fight a war, but it takes a smart man to jar any loose change out of any part of Europe. Especially when they have already eat up the money that was loaned them.

A Certain contemporary writer of Letters[13] claims eminence because he commuted back and forth to Europe at a time when the rest of the world was at war. His mission was easy. All foreign Nations wanted us to come in with them. All he had to do was to get us in, which he did. So his week-end voyages have no political significence at all, unless he be credited with an assist on the way to war.

But my mission will always stand out, because it is much easier for America to whip a Nation than it is for them to collect a dollar from them. I have to go abroad when we are as welcome as rent collectors. There is only one way we could be in worse with Europeans, and that is to have helped them out in two wars instead of one.

A few words might not be amiss as to why I was chosen. I will try and explain the whole thing in a few words, and I hope I do so in a way that will eliminate entirely my own personal achievements. I only relate them to show what I had done before being chosen by our President to embark on this mission to carry out my policies in his name.

I was born in Oologah, Oklahoma, near what then was the village of Claremore,[14] but which now embraces the entire northeast end of Oklahoma. From my earliest birth I was always doing things and letting other people get the credit. I started the Spanish-American War in '98. But I never said anything. I just sit back and let the Maine get the credit of it. I was the one who told Roosevelt[15] to call his regiment the Roughriders, even if there wasent a horse nearer Cuba than Lexington, Kentucky.

It was never publicly known only by a few intimates that I was really behind the election of Haskell[16] as the first Governor of Oklahoma. I also advised Al Jennings[17] not to run for Governor, as they would consider a Train Robber as an amateur in politics. I put Jack Walton[18] in and furnished the beef for the Barbecue. I managed Bryan's nomination Campaign in '96.[19] But on account of his losing the election, I have always claimed that I advised him strongly against running. I wanted him to be the only man that ever was nominated and then wouldent run. I dident do much backstage management until I advised Roosevelt to go ahead and run for Vice President, that something would turn up. We split over

Taft,[20] I wanted him to reduce and Roosevelt dident.

That brings my political advisement campaign down to the Wilson[21] election year. Well, it seems that he had someone doing the same style of work for him that I had picked out for my life's ambition. So I took up Tom Marshall[22] and it was through the way I handled him that he pulled Wilson through with him. The Republicans about that time made an offer in a black bag, and I layed the plans that Will Hays[23] so successfully reaped the benefit of in behalf of Harding's Campaign.[24]

The Democratic Convention of the early Twentieth Century was held much against my advice. I said they not only should not convene in New York City but that they shouldent convene at all; to save all their money and buy all the votes they could in 1928.[25]

Well, I was also the one that advised Coolidge to run on the Republican instead of the Democratic Party.

I don't care how unostentatious you do things, the news of them will gradually leak out. So, of course, naturally The President heard of me and my underground methods of doing things and that's how we got togeather. Now comes the most remarkable thing about our relation, and that is we have had no personal contact or agreement about taking up this work for him. In other words, our understanding has been so perfect between each other that we haven't even had to talk it over. There is a kind of mental telepathy between us.

I just felt that he needed a foreign Diplomat that could really go in and dip, and he dident even have to ask me to do it; that same intimate understanding that had told me he needed someone, had told him that I was the one that he needed. And that's all there has ever been between us. We just feel that our ideas are so mutual that whatever one does the other agrees with.

Of course we have foreign Ambassadors over there, but they are more of a Social than a Diplomatic aid to us.

Now I naturally in the course of human events had to communicate with my Master, and the following that you will read is the letters of a self-made Diplomat to his President.

We only had one understanding before I left and that was that everything between us must be carried on in an absolutely confidential manner, and not get out to the general Public. So it was decided to carry it on by postcard.[26] Just another example of typical American Diplomacy.

These letters had originally been given to the Reform School at Elmira, New York,[27] and it was through their generosity and ambition to aid future posterity that we are allowed to use them. We also want to thank the following who so generously and almost imploringly allowed us to use their names publically: Jack Dempsey, Peggy Joyce, Prince of Wales, Jim Furgeson, Lloyd George, Coley Blease, Hindenburg, Congressman Blanton, Mussolini and Annie Mc-Phearson:[28]

Letters of a Self-Made
Diplomat to His President

NEW YORK, April 28, 1926.

My Dear President: I was in Washington yesterday, but dident bother myself about coming around to see you. I was very busy. Our understanding is so antiseptic that I knew there was no use in talking over personally what I am to accomplish on this trip. Rest assured, My dear President, that your ideas are mine during this entire journey. I called at the Capitol to see what our hired help were doing. It's almost superfelous to tell you they were doing nothing. I wish we could get them interested in something. I have often thought a Book wouldent be bad, or do you think we could get them to read it? I wish you would give this some thought while I am away. Their mind, especially the Senate ones, are at a very plastic age now, and if we could get something started there, they might retain it; at least there is room anyway.

But, as I say, that is purely a local question and I seem to have no mind for small details. That can be taken up with Stearns any Sunday afternoon on the Boat.

I went in to see Dawes.[29] He is connected with one of our Departments there in a minor capacity. You might have heard of him, or heard him rather. If you dident shut both doors, you did, He was asking very anxiously after your health. I had to dissapoint him by telling him you were never better in your life.

He said the worry of the Presidential office had been to much for many of our Presidents. I told him I had never known a Vermonter to do any tremendous amount of worrying on $75,000 a year.

He just sighed, and we went on talking about something possible. I had a debt scheme that I told him off that I thought would have gotten us out with more money and more friendship than the course we have followed. It was this. Before anybody started to settle, why, let America agree on the lowest possible amount they could afford to take—that is, how much could they charge off. We will say, for example, we would be willing to take 50 cents on the dollar, at a small rate of Interest and to be collected over a course of years. Then announce to the World our terms; all the same, no favorites. Nobody would have any kick about the other getting better terms. That's the way a business does—finds out what it can charge off and does it and has it over with.

Well, Dawes agreed with me, and that showed right there that he is a pretty smart man. But he said that a funny thing was that

7

you couldent deal with Nations like you can with business men. That's on account of having what they call Diplomats. A Diplomat is a fellow to keep you from settling on a thing so everybody can understand it.

I had Lunch with Dawes. I would have come up to your house, but I dident know whether you had any help or not, and keeping

I told him I had never known a Vermonter to do any tremendous amount of worrying on $75,000 a year.

up a big house when you have always lived in a small one is quite a problem. Then I dident know but what you might charge me. Does Stearns pay Board or does he just live on you? I ate alone with Dawes. I was like Colonel House[30] when he agreed to see the Kaiser.[31] He only did it on condition that it be alone.

Well, that is the condition I implored when I was asked to dine with Dawes. The reason I did it was I dident want it to get out that I ate with a Vice President. You remember the trouble Roosevelt got in one time by letting everybody know who he ate lunch with.[32] After having eat with the Furgesons,[33] I dident want it to get out that I had got down to eating with only a Vice President. One thing, if it ever gets out, will be in my favor. They won't know who the Vice President was that I ate with.

But I am plain that way, and I know you are too. We don't either of us ever hold a man's low position against him. I remember one time you let a lot of Actors in there with you for breakfast. They had to stay up all night to be early enough for it. Now that was always a good example you set them. I think if more outsiders fed Actors we would have better acting. It's awful hard to do good acting on an empty stomach. And when they get back in there again during the next Presidential Campaign it will be another great thing. The only trouble is that once every four years is sorter scarce eating.

But to get back to Dawes and why I went slumming around with him. I wanted him to give me some tips on Europe. You know he was over there during the Dawes European Campaign.[34] He has two plans—his European Plan and his American Plan. The European one worked. I got along fine with him. I dident mention the words "Senate Rules." You know, if you get him off that subject he is pretty near sane as anybody. He surprised me. He eats right there in his office by the Senate door. He said he don't take any more chances on being caught asleep away down at the Willard.[35] He sleeps while he is presiding in the chair. He says Jim Reed[36] is his best nap.

Well, he gave me letters to everybody in Europe that was on that Dawes Plan over there with him. So if there is any little thing that he dident settle, why, I will take it up when I meet them. I hope he settled. After I left Dawes I went down to see Borah.[37] I mean Up to see Borah. We had quite a talk. I told him I was going to Europe. But I dident mention your name. I dident want to have to stop to explain who you were. I made him think that the trip would be in behalf of him. So he gave me a letter; just one of those "To Whom It May Concern." Now can you imagine me pulling that letter over in Europe—say, France for instance? I would be incarcerated in the Bastile from now hence. I asked him how he had everything running here in this country, and he said, "Oh, things are going along pretty good here now if some President don't butt in and spoil it. But in our foreign affairs, we meet and vote more money to Europe every day."

Went out to Alice's for dinner that night. Nick and the Wadsworths[38] were the other Guests. Alice asked how your strength was all over the country. I replied that outside of the Corn Belt you were pretty strong. She wanted to know why they couldent raise corn everywhere. Nick brought his Violin, but I got away before he could start to play. Jim Begg[39] called up while I was there and told Nick what time to be at work in the morning. Garner and Garrett[40] had quite a heavy schedule layed out for him the next day.

Wadsworth was worried more about the coming election than he was the welfare of the Commonwealth. He suggested I take Al Smith[41] with me to Europe. In fact he offered to defray the expenses of it if I would include a year's travel.

They all gave me an informal note to Ambassador Fletcher[42] at Rome, as I was desirous of being present at the next attempted[43] shooting in Rome. Alice and Mrs. Wadsworth and all of them informed me that[44] Fletcher was not a Stuffed Shirt. There is one for Slang hunters—you on Broadway and Main Street that think High Hat is the latest thing in the way of slang about a fellow who takes himself kinder serious. Alice comes to our rescue again with "Stuffed Shirt." Mrs. Wadsworth pulled a good one. She said, "Now you might be disappointed when you meet Fletcher. He wears Spats. But they don't go any further up than his ankle."[45] Well, we had a very pleasant time, as you can always have out there. And Alice also gave me a letter to Lady Astor over in the House of Commons in England. She is the Alice Longworth of England.

On leaving the Longworths I started to come by and see you; but it was nearly 9:30 and I knew you were in bed, so I went by Sol Bloom's[46] instead. Congressman Bloom was entertaining a big Party of distinguished friends, including the Members of the Italian Embassy, and they gave me letters to various officials in Italy, as I want to see this Mussolini. He is the Red Grange[47] of Europe now, and I want to see him before he turns professional.

The Minister from Greece was there. He wanted to know if I dident want to go to greece too. So if anything comes up here over the Restaurant situation that needs fixing, why, I am at your command to go immediately to Athens. A Cable "paid" will always reach me in care of the American Express Company.

Well, I got back to New York this morning, and that is about all of importance that I can think that happened yesterday. Have sent my laundry out and will be ready to sail Friday night on the Leviathan.[48] Have enough money, so don't bother Congress with another appropriation. But, however, will do as you say and draw on Melon[49] if necessary. Am going down today to get passport. Devotedly yours.

COL. WILLIAM ROGERS.

P.S. Am sending this Spaecial Delivery by Secretary New.[50]

NEW YORK, April 29th.

My Dear President: A matter come up which I think is of the gravest importance, and I think you should know of it, as it is things

10

of importance that I know you want me to find out for you. Well, I said I would like to get a Passport to go to Europe: "Here is the application and here is an affadavid that someone that we know will have to swear that they know of your birth and you will have to produce your Birth Certificate."

Well, I told her Lady I have no birth certificate; and as for someone here in New York that was present at my birth and can swear to it, I am afraid that will be rather difficult. "Havent you somebody here that was there?" she asked. You know the oldtime Lady's of which I am a direct descendant. They were of a rather modest and retiring nature, and being born was rather a private affair, and not a public function.

I have no one here in New York that witnessed that historical event, and I doubt very much if even in Oklahoma I could produce any great amount of witnesses. My Parents are dead, Our old Family Doctor, bless his old heart, is no more. So what would you advise that I do? Will it be necessary for me to be born again, and just what proceedure would you advise for me doing so? I remember Billy Sunday[51] once remarking to us just before a collection that "we must be born again," I dident take it so literally untill now. Billy had evidently been to Europe. You see, in the early days of the Indian Territory where I was born there was no such things as birth certificates. You being there was certificate enough. We generally took it for granted if you were there you must have at some time been born. In fact that is about the only thing we dident dispute. While you were going through the trouble of getting a birth certificate you could be raising another child in that time.

Having a certificate of being born was like wearing a raincoat in the water over a bathing suit. I have no doubt if my folks had had the least premonition at my birth that I would some day wander beyond any further than a cow can stray, they would have made provisions for a proof of birth. The only place we ever had to get a Passport for in those days was to go into Kansas. And I looked to have the average amount of intelligence of a child of my age and they knew that I would never want to go to Kansas.

Well, then the Girl finally compromised by saying, "Who here in New York knew your Parents? We know you, Mr. Rogers, but it's a form that we have to go through with before you can get the Passport. We have to have proof that you are an American Citizen."

That was the first time I had ever been called on to prove that. Here my Father and Mother were both one-eighth Cherokee Indians and I have been on the Cherokee rolls since I was named,[52] and my family had lived on one ranch for 75 years. But just offhand, how was I going to show that I was born in America? The English that I spoke had none of the earmarks of the Mayflower.

She asked, "Are you in Who's Who?"

I said, "My Lord, I am not even in the New York Telephone Directory, and that is perhaps without a doubt the most ordinary collection of humans ever assembled in America." I asked her, "Would you suggest waiting for a Passport until I have done something to get into Who's Who? If you do, I can see my trip to Europe fading. I will be dead of old age before making that Press sheet." But I was advised to go ahead and make out my application and that I

If you foreigners think it is hard to get in here, you ain't seen nothing. You ought to be an American and try to get out once.

would have to have a Picture of myself. She directed me to a place around there where I could get one taken quick. Well, that was the way I wanted one taken—quick.

The fellow as I walked in said, "Want to get mugged?" I replied, "Yes, sir."

"Sit down, hats off, heads up. You moved. I will have to shoot another one. Keep still."

My goodness, what speed! I thought I would get time to fix my tie or comb my hair, but not in that place. They shot you looking As Is. "How many do you want?" I asked him if I could see them first, as if by accident they were good I might take a dozen and have a Crayon enlargement made in addition.

I took the Pictures back and they pasted two of them on the passport and said, "$10.00 please." You see, with the application it cost you $10.00 to get out. In other words, they bet you $10.00 that you can leave the Country and you like a fool bet them that you can't. It's like betting a Life Insurance Co. that you will die, when they have every available information from Doctors and everybody that you will live. If it looks like you will die, they won't bet you.

Well, the Girl then said, "Now how about this sworn statement of someone who knows your Parents?"

Here is what I was up against: I not only couldent prove that I was an American but I couldent think of any other American in New York to vouch for me. It was as hard to find an American in New York as it was to get a Passport. I told the Lady, "If you think I wasent born here and will name me the country that you think I was born in, I will be glad to go there. It makes no particular difference to me where I go, so if you will just tell me where I might have originated from, why, that will be my destination."

You see, I was doing all in my power to be agreeable. So I finally went to a friend of mine—Sam Kingston[53]—assumed name—General Manager for Mr. Florenz Ziegfeld,[54] and I told him my troubles and he said, "Why, sure I knew your Father well, and I know that you are an American. Not 100 per cent ones like the Rotarray's and Kiawanises and Lions, but enough to pay taxes." Now Sam had never been west of the Hudson River in his life and my Father had never been east of the Mississippi, so it was really one of the longest distance acquaintanceships on record. I thought it was funny Sam had never mentioned knowing Father before to me. All he had ever spoken to me about was reductions of Salaries. Anyway I hope nothing comes of it in the way of hanging or shooting Sam.

So I took Sam's statement back and they won my $10.00. But one nice thing about the whole thing was the good nature and courtesy that the people in that Department showed—Mr. Hoyt, who was in charge, and Miss Baer and all of them. If it hadent been for them I would have felt like going out without one and trusting to luck to never get back again. So if you Foreigners think it is hard to get in here, you ain't seen nothing. You ought to be an American and try to get out once.

So as you sail down on the Mayflower tomorrow to keep away from the Congressmen I will be on the Leviathan with my oldest son[55] of 14—who is also a naturalized American Citizen. So as one Ocean traveler says to another, Bon Voyage, Calvin.

13

Yours cheerfully and well till we reach Sandy Hook.[56]
Your devoted Envoy without papers or sense.

COL. WILLIAM ROGERS.

April 30, '26.

My Dear President: Well, I guess you were getting kinder uneasy not hearing from me for last day or so. Well, after swearing I was American and getting Passports back from Kellogg[57] in Washington, I said to myself I am all set, now bring on your Europe. Then everybody all at once commenced asking me, "Did you get your Vesays?" I said no I never ate them, and dident care to take any along. Finally I had to tell one friend that I dident know whether I had them or not until I knew what they were.

Come to find out, a Vesay is nothing but getting your Passport signed by the Consul of the Nation where you want to go. But somebody in Europe called it a Vesay. I guess maby in their lingo it means signed, so naturally all Americans must speak of it as a Vesay. You could no more get an American that had ever been to Europe to say, "Did you get your Passport O. K. by the Consul?" than you could persuade him to jump out of the window. Oh, no, that is the one word he has learned in Europe and you certainly are not going to deprive him of the pleasure of speaking to you in a foreign tongue. He will go out of his way 10 times in his conversation just to get to say Vesay.

I would like to have you take that up, Mr. President, with some department in Washington and pass a law to have every American shot that don't speak to you as long as possible in our own language. It's bad enough to pay $10.00 for the Vesay without having your own people try out the word on you. You see, you pay $10.00 to get out of here; then you pay another $10.00 to get into the next place. I went to England's Consul and they Vesayed me out of 10 merry old iron men.

You see, the thing is a kind of a skin game. You pay the $10.00 over here. You don't know whether the Country you have paid the $10.00 to is worth that much to you or not. There is an awful lot of Countries that if they would let you wait till the boat pulled up there, and then you looked at them, you would decide right away, "This Joint ain't worth $10.00 to land in. Drive me on somewhere else."

Well, after England had got $10.00 of their debt money from me, I was what I thought all set, when someone said, "You are going to France, ain't you? Well, you might want to land in Cherbourg first, so go get your French Vesays."

14

By that time I was speaking the American Tourist language as good as they were. I knew what "Vesay" meant. So I went to the other end of New York to get an O. K. by the French. The Taxi bill was $4.80. That right there is a problem. It takes a pretty good country to be worth $4.80 nowadays.

Well, I will say one thing for the French—they dident monkey around. You handed them the $10.00 before you did the Passport. They dident seem to be particularly interested whether you got in their Country or not, but they sho did have an eye peeled for the 10 Bucks.

No wonder so many nations are dividing up into little ones over there.[58] Just think! They would Vesay you out of at least two thousand just to see all the Balkans. Some of those Nations, if they can get 10 visiting guests, can pay off their National Debt. I am supposed to get Germany's and Italy's and Spain's Vesays, but they are not going to get my 10 till I have to give it up. I am hoping that through the foreign rate of exchange I may be able to get a slight reduction on seeing some of them.

Being not what is proclaimed as a 100 per cent American, I went over on an American Boat. The 100 per centers all go on English or French, such as Hotel Men and Rotary Associations. It was to sail at 11:30 at night the last day of April. Oh, there was an awful lot of Jewish people on the boat. It looked like an old-time Follies audience. But there wasent a single Vesay for Palestine. I was the only one on the boat going there.

The Steamship officials said there was an extra-big sailing list. At twelve o'clock on May 1st, just 30 minutes after we sailed, the summer rates go into effect, and it costs you at least a third more. I being your Representative, I thought it would look bad not to take advantage of anything in the Economy line. Because it is only by our personal example that we can get people to follow our simple mode of living.

Oh, yes, I like to forgot—the boat was the Leviathan, the biggest and finest boat afloat. Manned by a real American crew. Every head officer is an American, without dialect. In 1914 I had been on this same boat on its first trip back across when it was the Vaterland and all the German officials had come over and back on it. And to show the difference as to how it was handled then and now, we backed out of the Hoboken docks at noon, in broad daylight, and went right on across the Hudson River and come pretty near knocking down the whole of Manhattan Isle; then sunk a tug on the way out. Well, this time we pulled out at midnight, and you wouldent know the thing was moving. Everybody received Flowers

15

and Fruit and Candy. We are just steaming down the bay. If you sent anything it hasent been sent to my stateroom yet. But there is a lot of Bundles and baskets up there yet that havent been delivered, and I will give you the benefit of the doubt till I find out otherwise. I will send this back by the Pilot. Hope it reaches you in time to offset the Cabinet meeting.

Yours devotedly,

COL. WILLIAM ROGERS.

P. S. Have you done anything for the Farmers yet?[59]

White House, Washington, D. C.

MR. CALVIN COOLIDGE:

Certain news is so urgent that it is nessary for me to cable you, so from time to time you may get something "Collect." I hope there is an appropriation to cover this, look under the heading "Ways and Means."

WILLROG (diplomatic code name) .

Radiogram.
SOMEWHERE IN THE
MIDDLE OF ENGLAND'S OCEAN.
Date ——— What's time to a guy in the
middle of an ocean.

My Dear President: Will you kindly find out for me through our intelligence Department who is the fellow that said a big Boat dident rock? Hold him till I return.

Yours feeble but still devotedly,

WILLROG.

That's code name for Will Rogers.

Latitude 7. Longitude 11.
Day of week still unknown.

My Dear Mr. President: I havent been able to do much physical investigation in your behalf, but between trips to the side and back to my chair I have been thinking of your best interests all the time. I have started my european tasks by calming the elements somewhat. I told the ocean that I would take it up with Congress and if nessasary appoint a Senate investigation if it continued its bucking and snorting around all over the place; so today it's as meek and docile as a Republican Convention.

I was just on the verge of having Captain Hartley[61] go ahead

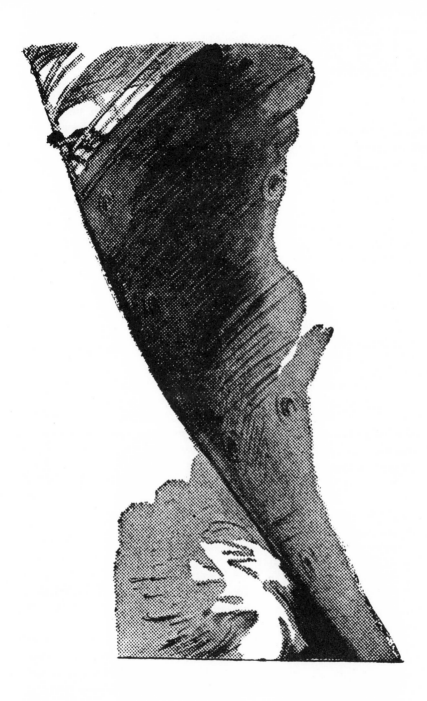

Will you kindly find out for me through our Intelligence Department who is the fellow that said a big boat didn't rock? Hold him till I return.

with a small boat and spread some Oil in our path, as I had heard that was an antidote for calm oceans. One day the U. S. Line, from a food standpoint certainly cleaned up. Nobody on the boat could say Dining hall, much less reach it. I heard quite a good deal of complaints as to why you can't travel on the European plan, and if there was no way to get a rebate. These are just little things, and perhaps I shouldent bother you with them.

But there has been a lot of little things come up on this trip— especially when it's rough[62]—and it has been so universal that I thought you should know of it and perhaps call an international conference if necessary.

Oh, yes, on this boat is a commission sent by you to go to Geneva to hold a preliminary Dissarmament Conference.[63] I have met all of them. They don't suspicion that I am going for you too, and I never let on. I just sit tight and listened. The Commission was headed by Mr. Gibson,[64] our Minister to Switzerland. I dident know we were sending Missionaries to Switzerland. Then I met him and found out he wasent a real Minister, but that it is a Title[65] in diplomacy.

Well, there was three of them from the Diplomatic end, three from the Army, headed by General Nolan and Major Strong,[66] and three from the Navy. Aviation—we dident send any over, because in case something broke out at home we might need both of the ... Well, they were all a fine bunch. There was two fine Rear Admirals—Admiral Hilary Jones and Admiral Andy Long.[67] On account of it being rough we dident see much of them. But when it cleared off everybody thought we had stopped somewhere and picked two new customers. Then we had as the third member of the naval forces your old Skipper Captain Andrews[68] of the old Republican Tug Mayflower. He was amazed at the size of the ocean, said he thought the old Potomac was big down around the mouth, but that this had it beat.

That was a splendid idea of yours, Mr. President, giveing those fellows some sea service like this; and even if the conference don't get anywhere, which it perhaps won't why this trip on the ocean will always be remembered by these three jolly old Salts. Allan Delles and Dorsey Richardson[69] were the other two candidates to help uphold Diplomacy with Mr. Gibson.

Now you are sending these fellows over there to talk about dissarming. Now just use your own judgement. Can you picture these Army and Navy fellows being enthusiastic for dissarming? Can you see Andy and Hilary voting a Battleship out from under themselves? It's a great move to passify the passafists, but these are pretty smart old Birds and they know when those boats will come in handy. And

18

General Nolan and Major Strong say if they give up anything it won't be anything more than their Spurs.

Just take your own case. Can you see yourself attending a Conference to abolish or even cut down Presidents? You might attend for propaganda sake, but you can bet your last maple tree you wouldent cut yourself down any or abolish the office. Can you see me attending a Lesser Chewing Gum Conference? The reason I bring this up is because there is no use in us kidding ourselves. It's all right to send Deligates and do a million and one things that the Public think amounts to something, but between us we know the whole thing is a lot of Apple Sauce. It's like, for instance, you meeting a Democrat and saying, "I am glad to meet you." Well, that has to be done. It is a custom. But of course, get right down to it, you are not glad to meet him at all. You are just human and wish there wasent such a thing.

Well, I am going by Geneva and see this thing. There will be 21 nations there, and outside of England and France and America, the others will take it serious. So I can just imagine the many quiet laughs those old Admirals will get out of that thing when somebody makes a speech about being no more war.

Commander Hartley of the Leviathan took me up on the Bridge and all over and showed me this wonderful boat. Between he and Moore and Higgins and the Chief Engineer, they manipulate this whole thing, big as the state of Rhode Island, while it is rooting its way across the Atlantic.

Here are some facts that might be of interest to you, Mr. President, as you were up in Boston at the time, and as you were having so much trouble with the Policemen[70] that I doubt if you heard just what the Leviathan was doing in the war. They transported hundreds of thousands of our men across and never lost a one. They have taken as many as 12 thousand at a trip. They slept in relays— that is, 8-hour shifts. Each bunk was slept in by three different men, 8 hours each. I would have liked to see somebody dig me out of my bunk the other day at the end of 8 hours, war or no war.

And there is something I bet you dident know, Mr. President: The Leviathan is the only boat that crossed without Convoy. She went it alone. She was faster than any Convoy and she figured on beating the Submarines by her speed and by taking a Zigzagging course. It's a great Boat and we ought to be proud of it. Talk about service! They make a sucker out of a Hotel.

You ought to come over some time. It used to be quite a fad for the President to run over for the week-end.[71] If you decide to come, let me know and I will give you a letter to Billy the Head

19

Steward. If you come on some of those French or other lines, you wouldent know what you were eating. Pancakes have got some crazy name. The trip would be over before you found out what they were.

Lot of Kids on the boat, including Fanny Ward.[72] But she dident have much fun. Her Grandparents were with her and they made her go to bed at nine every night. They were bringing her away from America, trying to break up a case between her and Jackie Coogan.[73] Marcus Loew and Lee Shubert,[74] the two biggest theater Owners in America, were on the boat. They both said they wished you would go to the Theatres more; that they thought it would have a good effect on the rest of the country. I told them a pass including Self and Party might have some effect on you. So if you get anything in the way of an Annie Oakley[75] in the next few weeks you will know that I am working in your interest every minute.

They publish a Newspaper on board that gives the amount murdered in Chicago every day. That and the ship's mileage run about equal.

Well, we got about in the middle of the ocean and the very thing happened that you and I have figured would happen, and that we talked about me fixing up in case it did happen. Well, it did. The General Strike in England.[76] We would get Radiograms from there every morning in the Papers and there was about 500 on there going to London, and they all switched and made arrangements to get off at Cherbourg, where we landed first. In fact the Captain got orders to have everyone get off there that possibly could. Everybody said, "Where are you going?" I told them I am going to London. Nothing is going to change me. I am on a mission and I want to show that I am a Soldier in the service of my country just as much as if I had on a uniform. Ain't that the thing they used to say? I think between you and I that it give a lot of men a chance to go to Paris whose wives had originally had 'em booked for England.

Everybody is getting off at six o'clock in the morning. But I am going on to London regardless of danger, because when one devotes themselvs to a cause, why, what is danger? I will follow lines in regard to strike that you suggest were so successful in Boston, and think that it will be only a few days till I have something to write you worth while.

Good night. Hope they haven't forced you too strong on that Farmer relief thing. That seems to be about the only thing they have been able to corner you in. Watch it both ways, because both sides vote.

20

We are just off France. I hear a noise. I thing it's the Franc dropping.

Your devoted accomplice,
COL. WILLIAM ROGERS.

London, British Empire, including Ireland.

May 6, 1926.

My Dear President: Owing to what they call lack of communication during the strike, I have been unable to reach you sooner with what I was doing. Now they say it was the strike that has slowed everything up over here, but personally I don't think it was the strike at all. In fact I think things are running faster. If I am not able to settle it, I am going to propose for the good of the country that they keep it going, for I feel sure that all Americans appreciate the change, and furthermore it gives an excuse. You know, England never had an excuse before for not getting anything done, but now they can lay it onto the strike. It's given them a topic. They never had a topic before. You know, they don't have Prohibition[77] over here.

But I must get back to where I left off over in Cherbourg. I got up early that morning and bid 'em all good-by. Made Captain Andrews promise me personally that he would do nothing at the Naval Dissarmament about scrapping the Mayflower. So don't worry about this summer. We will keep it till just before the Democrats get in the next time and scrap it then. Be a good joke on them, because they kinder take to the water anyway.

Another awful nice fellow on the boat was Garet Garrett.[78] I I think he does some Financial writing for *The Saturday Evening Post*. I dident know before that *The Post* ever sent men anywhere. I thought their stuff was just sent in by local Corespondents. I don't see how they could hardly afford to pay much, for it can't make much. They only get a nickel for it and it looks like there was that much paper in it. 'Course it picks up a little outside advertising, to get your mind off the reading, but that can't bring 'em in much. But he was traveling first class.

Then the day I left New York I met this fellow Issac Moccasin,[79] or Marcosin, or something like that. He works for that *Post* outfit too. He gave me a lot of letters to prominent men who he had interviewed,[80] and said they were still good friends of his. He spoke about you. I don't know how the name come up, in some roundabout way. He said he had interviewed about everybody, so maby that is how your name come up. He seemed very enthusiastic about

21

getting me to go to Russia.[81] He said he could get me in there; said they had been trying to get him back in there. He said he wasent doing anything now; said there was no one big enough to interview. I suggested that he just sit around and wait till the football season opened and write again about College Professors' salaries.

Well, Captain Hartley and I brought the Leviathan over to Southampton almost alone. Outside of some tugs that helped us dock and some men that helped unload and some busses and a train and some automobiles to take you to London, why, everybody in England was on strike.

I dident go ashore till the next morning and the American Express Co. had heard that I was doing some work for you and that my mission was official, so they had a big closed car there for me and my son, who is traveling as my Interpreter in England.

It's about 80 miles through the most beautiful Country you ever saw up to London; every field planted and plowed and raising something. And by the way there is no Farm relief problem over here. This is only a suggestion and I doubt if it could be carried out, but I think some work on those Farms over home wouldent be a bad solution to their problem. These fellows looked like they had solved their Farm problems by working on them. I won't be certain, but I think that's it.

You see, they have figured out the Jimson weeds and Cockleburs and Sunflowers and all kinds of weeds take up as much room and as much nourishment out of the ground as wheat or oats do, so they just don't raise them. They will pull 'em out with their hands if they have too. The trouble with our farmers is that they raise too many things they can't sell. These only raise what they plant there to raise. But they ought to raise more over here; they have more time. They don't drive to town till they drive in to sell something. Gloria Swanson[82] proving that virtue will triumph in the end is taken as a matter of fact. They don't have to go every night to see it proved. Leaving the field and going to a Lions' Luncheon is another thing they have never figured as an actual farmers' accomplishment toward less weeds and more Porridge.

Just imagine! I was in a Farmer's house here and he and his family had a Book instead of a Radio. These are just little suggestions when the Farm relief Associations wakes you that might not be amiss to you every morning up.[83]. Of course one thing that makes for economy over here that you have to reckon with over there is the Garage question. Their car and their wagon here is generally under the same shed, even if it's only big enough to hold one.

All along the road there was Soldiers and Armored Trucks. I

thought at first on account of me being on unofficial business that I was being convoyed. But they had been put there to keep order. So the strikers and the Soldiers were all sitting around chatting and having Lunch together. Mind you, there was five million men out on strike out of a total Population of fifty million. We drove clear into London and never saw one bit of excitement. Everything that is running is only about at one 5th of its regular strength. Not a Newspaper. Just a little double sheet that looked like it had been printed on a Typewriter. Looked about like the Congressional Record on a day when they retire early.

London, May 12, 1926.

When I'd been in London a while I said to myself, I got to do or see something or I will bust. I says I will go into the House of Commons—or Parliament, rather. I have seen it now and I prefer calling it the House of Commons. Well, as I say, I had a terrible lot of letters from everybody but you, and you know one of the beautiful parts of our friendship and understanding with each other is that we seem to know without all the ordinary connection that others would have. But it's just perfect coördination between us.

I started to see about getting into this House of Commons, and after getting into association with even the head of the Associated Press, he said, "Why, Lord, I can't get in there myself!" So I was advised to go to the foreign Press office to a Sir Somebody-or-other. Well, I sent in my name and the fellow come back and said, "He will see you presently." I then waited about an hour.

When Sir finally come out, I said "Strike is on here, ain't it?" Well, that one was lost on the Sir, and I had thought it was pretty good. It was the best one I could think of in a hour's time. Well, he took me over to another man and I showed him my Press credentials where I was writing for the Claremore Progress, of Claremore, Oklahoma. The minute they saw that they not only gave me the pass but asked all about Claremore; said they had always been interested in the marvelous development of the town, and that it had often been suggested that they send men from London to study our method of running the town.

You see, I knew I would have to wait and delay with this first man when I found out he was a Sir. Now afterwards I mixed with Lords and even the Prince, but these Sirs are toughest birds there are to get to. You see, Sir is about the lowest form of Title there is. It's the Ford of Titles, it's just like it is over home—if you want anybody, find the owner. Be leery of Secretaries and Vice Presidents

23

of Business concerns. They are like the Sirs. It's their first importance. I can go talk to Henry Ford,[84] but I would hate to have to
do it through his Secretary.

Well, after I got my pass I started in to try and get in the Gallery. Say, I wish you could see the amount of Policemen and people
that had to Vesay that document. I just thought shades of Jim Preston[85] in our Press Gallery in the Senate. Why, he has to go out and
draft fellows to go in and listen to our gang. A pass? Why, over home
we will give you a meal if you will go in and listen. And as for Policemen, there is only one on duty in that whole end of Washington.
If you are going to have a lot of Policemen around, how are the
Bootleggers going to get in—without splitting?

I just said to myself, this Commons better be good after I have
wasted this day on it and ain't it yet. If there was five million men
on strike, there was five million others working, trying to keep you
out of the house of Commons. The last guy had a dress suit on at
2:30 in the afternoon, and I had always been led to believe that
Englishmen knew how to dress. I thought my goodness if he had a
dress suit on now, I guess if they hold a night session he will have
on Pajamas. He planted me in what was known as the Foreign Press
department. It was a good seat to see anything, if there had been
anything to see.

Well, they met, and a man who was just engaged for that business prayed.[86] He incidentally mentioned the King more than he
did the subjects. That struck me as kinder odd, because from what
I had seen of the King and the house he was living in, and what
I had seen of the subjects, I thought the King was doing pretty
well, and dident particularly need any help. At least, to be fair, I
thought the Subjects should have an even break.

But I am not one to go around criticizing anything connected
with religion. If you knew enough to keep out of the Klan fight,[87]
I certainly ought to know enough to not mix up in any of England's
religious prayers. I am not the fellow to go a Country and then
start criticizing it from our angle at home. You have to look at a
thing through their eyes to be fair.

Now over in the House of Lords it is different. They have an
outsider come in there every day and pray for them. One man
couldent do enough praying for them. But it can't just be the ordinary Preacher. He must be an Archbishop. You have to have
had a lot of praying experience to know just what their wants and
needs are. The day I was in their Joint, why Archbishop of Canter-
burry[88] prayed for them. It was at a particularly momentous time
and they needed some mighty pretty praying, so they called in the

24

best there is in all of England. And the funny part about it to any of you nonbelievers is that in three more days the strike was settled. So I am going to suggest him for the Democrats just before the next election. They could bring him over on some other mission so it wouldent just look too obvious. They could make this Democratic want prayer kinder look like a side line. The only thing is if he enumerated all the Democrats' needs he would be kept out of London too long.

But it's not of the House of Lords that I am talking to you now; it is of the House of Commons. Well, this Commons dident lose

They are rude in the Commons—they holler at each other and interrupt and yell.

25

any time about getting down to the strike. If it had been over home and a strike had been on all over the Country, they would have met and argued Prohibition. Finally Lloyd George got up. He belongs to what is called the Liberal Party, whose standing is now about what the Populist Party[89] is in America. I sho was glad to be there and hear him. He was criticizing the Paper.

You see, when the strike started, the Government put out this one little paper. This Archbishop of Canteburry had offered a means of settling the strike, but the paper dident use it. The Government dident want to make any surrender of any kind. Well, the Union Party on the other side—they are what the Republicans are, if they all stuck together over home—they got to hooting and riding Lloyd George. Well, that dident seem hardly right to me. Here was a man that had brought them through the most critical times in their History as Prime Minister, and now they rode him just because he happened to degenerate into a common Member of Parliament—M. P.—that's about like you, Mr. Coolidge, being in Congress after you had been all these years in the White House.

Now, as I say, I dident like that. That was the only thing I saw in the English that I dident like. The man felt bad enough by having to belong to the house of Commons, much less them trying to rub it in on him. Just picture yourself sitting up there between Blanton and Upshaw[90] and you will realize about how I felt about Lloyd George that afternoon.[91] He dident like it either. He was talking and somebody hollered out, "What Party are you doing this talk for?" You see, there is also a Labor Party in there, too, who were in favor of the strike, because they wasent doing anything themselves, so five million more men joining them dident mean anything.

Lloyd George said, "I am doing it for no party. I am doing it as a British Citizen, and I think I have done enough for this Country to command some respect."

Say, Boss, he knocked 'em for a voting booth with that. They listened to him till he got through. You see, it was just like it is over home. It was such a novelty to hear a man be for his Country instead of his party that it was a novelty. Lloyd George showed some of the old-time fire that they say used to make 'em all bring sticks out of the water for him. He just let 'em know that he knew it was almost a disgrace to be in there with them in Parliament, but that he deserved something better anyway.

Well, about this time up in the Gallery a couple of young Guys come climbing over everybody, stepping over seats, and planted themselves right down in the middle of the front row. I thought, "My Lord, is Yale turned out?" Finally everybody was craning their neck to see, and these two turned to speak to each other, and who do you think one of them was? Not a soul that amounted to anything but the Prince of Wales. I thought, shades of Long Island and no sleep all summer, if that ain't the Kid himself! He was about three or four rows in front of me.

But to make sure that it wasent my eyesight and not the lack of Prohibition, I said to someone sitting in close proximity—that means not far away, in English—"Who's the two youths that have just crashed the gate?"

He answered me out loud, but pitied me internally: "That's the Prince of Wales." I then asked, for when ignorance gets started it has no bounds, "Who's the Boy friend with him?"

"That's the Duke of York."[92]

I said, "Is that all it is? I thought they were particular over here in England who the Prince run around with."

Well, all I got for that gag was a hard look. I felt like hurdling right over these few rows and asking the Prince if he ever remembered a Country called[93] America. Then I happened to think of all those Policemen, and, having just seen the Tower of London and where they beheaded people that just tipped their hat at a wrong angle to a King, I said to myself, "Willie, be calm or the U. S.[94] will lose one of their annual annoyances." I wasent afraid of him. I knew he would be all right. But I have seen Guys get practically exterminated before someone is able to explain.

When I finally got my eyes off the Prince why, Winston Churchill[95] was answering Lloyd George. It seems that he is what they call the Home Secretary and was responsible for this little E-flat Pamphlet that the Government had been putting out under the humorous name of a Newspaper. He explained to Lloyd George that it was very hard, as some connected with the paper had never been in a Newspaper office before; and some Laborite hollered out, "Including the Editor." That was what I would call a real Nifty, and, say, it went over with a bang. Any time you think these English haven't any humor you are cuckoo. You see, Winston was the Editor, and that kinder halted him a few seconds. The Prince laughed. Even you would have had to laugh at that, Mr. President.

Finally somebody with no reputation got to making a speech and it was just like over home—everybody walked out. The Prince left so fast I thought there was a dance announced somewhere. Well, down among these 600 men was one lone woman, the first one ever to sit in this great body of Lawmakers. And here she was American Born and Raised. There she sit in the most modest little black dress with just a little white about the collar. I saw her write a note and in a few minuees I saw her at the side of our Gallery and was handing the Note along the front row and it was for the Prince.

Well, when I saw that happen I thought I wonder what could be between those two. She is much older and a married woman with a large family. Then that reminded me of something. I had among all my gripful of letters one from Mrs. Astor's Sister and Brother-in-law in New York, Mrs. Chas. Dana Gibson.[96] You know, they were the famous Langhorne Sisters of Virginia, all beautiful and accomplished. Well, they all did wonderful in marriage. Even the one that married Charles Dana Gibson dident do so bad at that. He has more humor and more money than any Artist that ever drew a Picture. And Mrs. Gibson, I remember the last time I saw her I tried to assist her at a big Luncheon to try and get people to adopt more babies. The Luncheon was a failure as far as I was concerned. I offered three little heathen if anyone would take them, and didn't get rid of a one of them. You can always get rid of children easier if the people don't know who the Parents are better than if they do.

I went down below and sent this letter in to Mrs. Astor. That took one hour and a half and 1 pound, 3 shillings and 6 pence. But the letter was so informal and it was written as though you really wanted the people that you were introducing to meet. Say, she come a-bursting down one of those old stately halls of Jurisprudence and made me feel like my seasickness had not been in vain.

She heard me talk, and the first word was "Boy, where did you get that Nigger dialect? It sho sounds like home to me."

Well, she was no more Lady Astor—or what her title really is is Vicountess—that's better than a Lady— she was just Mrs. Astor to me, and she would be to any American that ever met her. My goodness, what a relief to meet somebody that was natural and just themselves again! She had a position, but she dident feel called upon to uphold it every minute. She seemed to think that it would get along without her defending it every second. Some Lady was there dragging her off to talk to a big bunch of Sailors. She said, "Come on with me. You ain't doing anything." Well, she certainly had it right—I wasent doing anything, especially if she wanted anything done. On the way down, she said, "I don't know what to do for these boys. Say, can't you say something to them? Can you talk to people?"

So you see I had no reputation that had preceded me. She was nice to me just because I was an American. She might even have took me for a Senator. She is just that nice that she would be likely to treat one of them civilly.

I said, "Anything to please you. I will try and speak a few words in public, although I may faint."

Well, say, I am not kidding you. I had a tough time following her on that program. She kidded the boys and told 'em jokes and she was a riot with them. She dident have to go to England to get in Politics. She could have stayed right in Virginia and Carter Glass[97] would have been running his Newspaper in Lynchburg, for she would have been the Senioress Senator from the Commonwealth of Virginia. What a team her and Alice Longworth are when it comes really to savying politics.

Well, I unlimbered a lot of old Sailor jokes. All I had to do was to change them from the American to the English Navy, which dident take any great amount of intelligence. Well, the boys were great, and if I had gone that good in some of my Lecture Towns this last year I might have got a return date. Well, then nothing would do but I must tell Members of Parliament and a lot of her friends all these Political wheezes.[98] I want to tell you what all happened in the next few days, how these English people acted through all this trouble. Honest you wouldent think a people could be so cool. From the time it started to the time I ended it, as per your instructions, there was not a shot fired. Think of that!

Say, I would have liked to brought 10 Chicago Taxi Drivers over here and showed them a strike! London would have thought the late war was on again. They are a great people in a crisis, these English. It would have been worth for an ad all the strike cost them if the rest of the world could have been there and seen it. There was no such thing as a strike breaker as we know them. Everybody just pitched in and carried on the work. Every private car going along was at your disposal if you were going some place, at no cost at all.

Colleges like Oxford and Cambridge turned out and they did police duty or run engines on the railroads or drove busses. I think even the Lords took up some useful occupation. And here to me, Mr. President, was the greatest thing of all: Not a striker ever did a thing to interfere with any of them even if they were trying to do the strikers' old jobs.

The House of Commons and the Americans there were the only unruly ones. They are rude in the Commons. They holler at each other and interrupt and yell. That's the only ungentlemanly conduct I saw in all England during the strike. Oh, yes, and the house of Lords. I will have to tell you about that later. They dident even know the strike was on at all, it was so far removed from them. When it was over, there was no jubilation or hollering. It was just as quiet and calm as it had been during it. I was in the House of Parliament when the Premier announced that it had been settled.

You know, along with this business of settling everything over here, I have to have some recreation, so I am going out and see something. There is a lot of wonderful new Shows here—Is Zat So? which by the way is a riot; No, No, Nanette, Mercenary Mary, Kid Boots, Student Prince, Lady Be Good.[99] I just wish we had Abie's Irish Rose[100] here to make me feel perfectly at home. They say there is one of those Companies of it coming over here next year just as soon as their run is over at Albuquerque, New Merico.

Paul Whiteman[101] is over, and so is Fritz Kreisler.[102] Funny to have two fiddle players here at once, ain't it? But that is just the way

If they had just punctured the bicycles, that would have stopped traffic dead.

they do things. Even run their traffic the wrong way. No wonder they are always having trouble. Look at us! We can't run ours and we make 'em turn out for each other the right way.

There is only one way they could ever have made this strike a success from a transportation standpoint and that is if they had just Punctured the Bicycles. That would have stopped traffic dead.

Havent heard from you after cabling you Collect about stopping strike? Where will I go for the next bit of work? Poland has got a home-talent war on. Will I go stop that or just let 'em wear themselvs out? I heard Paderwriski[103] played the Piano while Warsaw burned.

30

Well, I will stop. If this seems long and tiresome and nonsensical to you, why, never mind reading it. Just introduce it into Congress as a Bill and they will pass it.

Your devoted servant,
Col. William Rogers.

P.S. If you help the Farmer, remember what I tell you. Be careful at who's expense you help him.

London, May 13th.

My Dear President: Say, I told them about you over here. During all this calm and no excitement, everybody asked me, "How would you Americans take this if it were happening over there?"

So I just told them: "We would have all been cuckoo and crazy and shooting and rioting, and everybody up in the air—all but one man. He would have been just like your House of Lords. He might every few days ask, 'Is the strike over yet?' But he would have been the sole individual that would have not turned a hair."

Then they all would ask, "Who is this remarkable man that you speak of?"

I remarked, "Calvin Coolidge."

I wish you had been there. It was just your kind of stuff. Oh, yes, I met Houghten,[104] our Ambassador, at a Dinner Party at Mrs. Astor's. Sat next to him. I will write you later and in more confidential terms just how he is making out over here. Don't think there is any need for a change of men here now. If Kellogg should decide to get out, I think this fellow would be the man to put in there. You know, we have always used this court of St. James's as a kind of a springboard to dive from into the Secretary of Stateship, and from there to oblivion. I am watching him, and believe I can get Borah to O.K. him when the time comes.[105]

I will go and see if London Bridge is falling down. I have heard somewhere that it was.

Yours as ever,
W. R.

P.S. Watch the farmers. They are tricky.

London, May 16, '26.

My Dear President: I was going to write you sooner, but after being here a week or more I commence to get just like the British. You must always say British. If you say English, why, Ireland, Wales, Scotland and the dominion provinces won't like it. So it's always The British.[106]

The strike was carried on something like this: Some government man would approach a man and ask, "Could I get you to drive a

Tram for us? We are really in great distress at not being able to perambulate."

"No, sir, I can't drive it for you; I am on strike. I am a Tram driver by profession. However, I should be very glad to assist you if it's not presuming too much on your short acquaintance. I will see who I can find that is not on strike and send them around to you."

"Well, that's very nice of you, old chap. It's deucedly awkward to have to approach a strange man and ask him to assist you without at least a previous introduction. But on learning that you were a

"No sir, I can't drive for you; I am on strike."

striker I knew that you would be in sympathy with my position and do all you can to assist me in this awfully embarrassing position of having to ask a perfect stranger for aid. Here is my Card. I don't like to hasten you, but I should be very much obliged if you would get me the man as quickly as he is procurable. Beastly old Tram and everything; looks awfully unsightly just standing there not doing anything."

"I shall have a man there in 'alf a mo', gove'nor, I shall even tell him 'ow to run the blooming thing if he 'appens to be a college man and don't know anything sir."[107]

The whole thing from both sides was handled like a well-organized Funeral, by an old well-established Undertaker. There wasent a hitch. The Undertaker, in the guise of the Government, just slipped on the old white gloves and strolled casually through the entire procession. The Strikers, in the guise of the corpse, dident make a kick or a holler. He was just there to furnish the cause; he wasent there to change British procedure even in strikes.

The thing got on my nerves so that, although I am not a man that particularly craves excitement, I wished they would drop the Corpse, or that he would suddenly come to life and kick out the top of the glass or something—anything for a change. But He dident and they dident. Everything went just as scheduled.[108]

I just thought as I watched this day after day, Oh, if two dogs would only fight! And mind you, Mr. President, I am not a man that likes Dog fights. I love dogs and I hate to see 'em fight each other. But if a man had put on a Dog fight and charged admission, he would have had every American in London there, including the entire Humane Society, just for one teeny speck of excitement. I wish I could have mustered up a little more nerve. I would have busted somebody in the jaw just to see what would have happened. Not that I had it in for anybody or either side, but you can only stand so much.[109]

But if you are going to do a strike over home you either do it or don't do it; don't advertise it and then not go through with it. If you Bill anything as such in the papers over there you got to put it on. So all I blame England for was the Billing. It should have been called A Temporary Cesession of Employment without Monetary Consideration for an Indefinite Period, Without Animosity or Hostile Design.

Now with that kind of advertising no one would have had a speck of complaint. That would have covered the case thoroughly. But a Strike! My Lord, it wasent even in three feet of the Plate. Not even a Cockeyed American League Umpire could have called that a strike. I saw a crowd assembled and I rushed over to see what the excitement was all about, and it was two Strikers helping a Strikebreaker fix a puncture on a Bus.

The only excitement caused was by a young fellow who had volunteered to run a train as Engineer. He got it out to a Station and couldent get it started again. Finally, as all the passengers were in their seats waiting, he come back along the coaches and hollered out, "Is there anybody here knows anything about an Engine?" Boy, he emptied that train right then when they found he was the one running it.

You see, the hard thing in this whole strike, from an American standpoint, is to look at an Englishman and judge from the way he is working whether he is on Strike or not. Now you take Tea time, for instance. There is not an American that wouldent say England is on strike. But they wouldent be at all; it would only be Tea time. That is why the strike looked so small. There was only five million out on it, but at Tea time there is 51,683,423 on strike. You see, that is why

33

it is so hard to excite people that are used to that much leisure every day, anyway, whether there is a Strike or not.[110]

And by the way, Mr. President, who owns Coal mines anyway? There is always trouble in the coal mines, both over home and here, and nobody knows who the Coal Mine Owners are. In any other Industry we all know who owns it and we know that he will go out and deal with his men. For instance, the Automobile. If there was a strike in that whole Industry, we would know that Henry Ford and Irskine and Willys[111] and all of them would go to the workers and lay their cards on the Table and show them just what they were making and what they were able to pay, and it would never get any further. They could settle it, and we would look to them to settle it, and blame them if they dident.

But the Coal owners—nobody knows who they are, and why they can't go and deal with the men that work for them, and fix them so they will have confidence in the owners like other lines of work have in the men they work for. The Miners can't be wrong all the time. In fact their wages don't prove that they are a lot of Plutocrats. So let's find the mine owner in both countries and see just what type of man he is, and who he is. Nobody should be allowed to employ labor that can't deal with them Personally. So kindly take this up at the next Cabinet meeting and see what we can do about it.

I believe there are thousands of people over ,home and perhaps in England that would be just like me. I would like to know who these mythical people are, the Mine Owners.

I bet Charley Schwab[112] or dozens of other men they have either in America or England could take their Coal Business, the whole thing, and in six months have the men working the mines and offering to Caddie for him for nothing. Maybe they would be getting only a dollar a day, but they would feel that they were getting every cent the Coal Business could afford to pay them. We have spent twenty years blaming the Miners, so let's find out who these Owners are and look them over and see if they are all Cannonized.

Well, I must close. Here comes the Postman. I want to see his funny Cap. Hope I hear from you on what is doing on your end. I only hope you have done as well there as I have been able to do here. If I do say it myself, I have handled Lloyd George admirably during this trouble over here. Can you say as much for Borah? Well good-by for the present.

Your devoted manservant.

W. R.

CALCOOL, *Washhousewhite:*

LONDON, May 17.—Don't put too much faith in rumor that peasants of Middle West will defeat you.

They change with the wheat crops, and you have two to go.

Yours politically,

WILLROG.

Tower of London, London.[114]

May 17, '26.

MY DEAR MR. PRESIDENT:

I been hearing rumblings of rumors now.

Just how is things breaking over there anyway? Some papers we get over here say you are sorta skidding on the turns and they look for you to throw a tire in the home stretch. Other papers of opposite form of public insanity claim that it is just a little natural reaction setting in, that a man can't go on high every minute; that he has to sorter slow up and look back every once in a while to see if anybody is getting close to him. Course, there has been a lot of races lost by looking back at the wrong time.

They claim that the farmers are kinder losing confidence in you helping them out. Well, you are pretty wise; you know there ain't many Farmers. There is an awful lot of people farming but if it's only the FARMERS that are against you, why, you haven't lost much strength. You got to do more than just live in the country to be a Farmer.

Then again you got to figure that it's a long time till the fall of '28. A couple of good crops and any fair luck working along the line of supply and demand, and you will capture the Farmers back again. You know rain in Iowa, an Epidemic of Appendicitis among the Boll-weevil, or fallen arches on the Chinch Bugs, all play just as big a part in the national career of a man as his executive ability does.

You give me a few showers just when I need them most and let me have the privilege of awarding them around among the doubtful states as I see best; let a certain demand for steel crop up which I didn't even know was going to crop; let the Argentine and Russia have a wheat failure; let the foot and mouth disease hit every country out west of the Mississippi; let, as I say, all these things happen over which I have no direct control, and have even me in there as President, and I will be reelected by such a large majority that I won't even take the pains to talk to you over the rodeo.

Give me all those things for 10 years in succession with me as President and I will give Lincoln a run for his laurels, even if I can't spell cat, and eat with my knife, and don't know a tariff bill from a Tee Bone Steak.

Being great as President is not a matter of farsightedness; it's just a question of the weather, not only in your own Country but in a dozen others. It's the elements that make you great or that break you. If the Lord wants to curse about a dozen other Nations that produce the same thing *we* do, why then you are in for a re-nomination. If we are picked out as the goat that year and are to be reprimanded, why, you might be Solomon himself occupying the White House and on March the fourth you would be asked to "call in a public conveyance and remove any personal belongings that you may have accumulated." So it's sorta like a World Series—you got to have the breaks.

Everybody figures Politics according to what they have accumulated during the last year. Mayby they havent earned as much as they did a few years ago, because they haven't worked near as hard, but all they look at is the old balance sheet and if it's in the RED why his Honor the President is in the alley as far as they are concerned. It takes about 20 or 30 years to really tell whether any President really had anything with him beside Sunshine and Showers. We have to look over your achievements in view of what they have to do with the future, of course, bad advice will ruin you just about as quick as total Earthquake all over the land would, if you are trying to be elected and then listen to a typical Politician or a bunch of them (for there is nothing as short sighted as a Politician unless it is a delegation of them.) Well, if you are going to pay any attention to Politicians during your administration you can just right away imagine yourself being referred to as "Ex-President Jasbo." They, I really think, can ruin you quicker than unseasonable weather.

Now, your personal habits, your looks, your dress, whether you are a good fellow or not with the boys, the old assumed Rotary or Kiwanis Spirit, why that don't mean a thing. You can shut up and never say a word for the entire four years; you can go out and talk everybody deaf, dumb and blind; you can be a teetotaller; you can have a drink whenever you like—in all these things and a million others you can be either on one side or the other and it won't make the least bit of difference in the world, if the Country has enjoyed prosperity, over ninety percent of which you had no personal control.

Every Guy just looks in his pockets and then votes, and the funny part of it is it's the last year that is the one that counts. You can have three bad ones and then wind up with everybody having money, and you will win so far you needn't even stay up to hear the returns. You can go to bed at 10:30. On the other hand you can get a great break and give them a great first three years of your incumbency and then the last or election year flop on account of a drouth and you will be beat so far they will think you was running as a Wet.

So that's how much all these write-ups and Editorials amount to. They haven't got any more to do with conditions in November '28 than Idaho has advising Borah.

In Politics, as well as in anything else and even more so, you have to sorta bet or play on a man's luck. Take Golf, for instance. Hagen[115] they will tell you can't play as good a game as Bobby.[116] But you let there be a few hundred beans in a bag that has been wagered on the outcome and Hagen will make the last 10 holes in ONE each. Now they may think they can outgeneral you but let them look up your record and they are going to have a tough time out lucking you.

That guy, Smith, is another guy that carries Horseshoes where poor Bryan never had anything on his person but Peacock feathers.

Now, mind you, I am granting all of you the same ability. But it's the four leaf clover that brings home the bacon. So don't pay any too much attention to anything till I get there, and confer with you personally. They say you must have the tide with you to swim the Channel. Well, you certainly have to have the weather with you to keep on being President.

Good wishes for many more happy returns of Innaugarations,

Your "Dug-out" in Europe,

WILL.

Special Cable

CALCOOL, *Whitehousewash:*

LONDON, MAY 18.[117]—You can pick an American bootlegger out of a crowd of Americans every time. He will be the one that is sober.

Yours temperately,

WILLROG.

WHITE HOUSE, WASHINGTON, D. C.

May 8, '26.

WILLROG, Savoy Hotel, London.

[Secret code name for Will Rogers]

My Dear Will — — —— —— —— —— —— ——

———— ———— ———— ———— ———— ———— ———— ———— ————

Yours truly,

The PRESIDEN.

[code name for President]

LONDON, May 18, '26.

My Dear President: Yours received and contents noted. You don't know how glad I was to receive your newsy letter. It certainly did feel good to have all the news of the Old Country again. Your letter made me feel like I was right there and hearing you say all those things,

37

and it really made me homesick. You don't know how I appreciate you taking the time off from all your many busy chats you have with everybody over there to tell me all these little trifling details like you did.

After meeting Mrs. Astor, as I told you about in a previous communication, and playing the show for the Sailors with her, why, she wanted me to give my idea of the way the strike should be settled to a lot of her friends and fellow M.P.'s. This is not meant for Mounted Policemen, as you would naturally interpret it, but it's for Members of Parliament. To be a Mounted Policeman you have to stand a very rigid examination both mentally and Physically, and serve a very rigid apprenticeship for the position; while with the other M.P.'s there is no requirement necessary. Well, she gave a Dinner in the House of Parliament and was good enough to have me come and meet several of the Leaders. She said, "Your plan of settlement will cheer them up. We are in the midst of this horrible strike and everybody feels depressed."

Well, personally, I could see no more depression on their faces than had ever been there in any of my other visits to England. She was, generous soul that she is, trying to lay this depression—or suppression rather—on the strike, while I knew that it was the breeding. It was the outcome of generations. It wasent the strike was doing it; it was Nature.

Well, we had an awful nice Dinner; and when I tell you, Mr. President, that there was several glasses to every plate, and not a speck of water nerer than the Thames, it suggests what is being done right under the very house-top of that great Law-making Body. Why, you would have thought a bunch of Senators were in a private room of a Washington hotel instead of right out in the open in the House of Parliament. And here was men like these in charge of the destinies of a great Nation, including Ireland and Scotland.

But I am tickled to tell all our Dry friends over home that Mrs. Astor personally is an ardent Prohibitionist; and when she saw me refuse a drink that was so strong that the waiter had to wrap it up in a towel to keep it from blowing up, why, it seemed to please her very much. Then I pulled the thing that is an unforgivable sin in England or Europe— I asked for water. Well, that is just like asking for Prewar Beer over home. They have everything else, but nothing dissrupts a well-organized Dinner outside America as much as to have some Bonehead ask for a glass of water. It is just used for raining purposes every day in England.

Well, Mrs. Astor thinks that Prohibition has been a big thing toward American present-day prosperity, and I met no one in England who I value their opinion any more on any subject than this same American woman. But she is broad-minded enough to not try to remedy the country single-handed.

Well, now these M. P. fellows there in the room at the dinner, they were just about like a bunch of old Nesters elected to congregate at Oklahoma City, or Austin, or Bismarck, every two years. They were

Nothing disrupts a well-organized dinner outside of America as much as to have some Bonehead ask for a glass of water.

just about like those old Birds over home. They were just spending this term trying to get back the next. The welfare of the country generally felt a little heavier around there November fourth. But I liked them and I like those over home. We cuss 'em and we joke about 'em, but they are all good fellows at heart; and if they wasent in that, why, they would be doing something else against us that might be worse.

There was another outsider at the Dinner besides me that Mrs. Astor told me she wanted especially for me to meet, and she sit him right by me, and what a wonderful little man he is, and meeting him will always remain one of the high spots in my memory.[118] It was Sir

James Barrie.[119] I think he is a Syndicate writer, or Strip Cartoonist, or Paragrapher, or something like that. I think he had a Cartoon running called Peter Pan, and a little Comedy Character called the Little Minister. They were afterwards made into Books.

Well, we had a great time. Now can you imagine me sitting down beside Sir James Barrie? Stop here and laugh at the idea of it. I did when I saw it, so you have nothing on me.

He said, "Are you a Writer?"

Well, that did bring the big Guffaw. I had to bust right out at that. He was such a nice and pleasant little man that I wanted to be honest with him and tell him no. Then I happened to think of the three typewriters I had worn out, and I wasent going to give up without a struggle. The strikers might give in, but not me.

So I said, "Yes, Sir, are You?"

He said, "No."

I said, "Well, I am, if you ain't, because we are certainly opposite."

He said, "What did you write?"

I said, "Tobacco Ads."[120]

Then I asked him what he wrote and he said Peter Pan.

And then he said, "I should like to read your ad book." Well, come to find out, Mrs. Astor had of course tipped him off to me, and the Rascal was kidding me all this time. But, anyway, we broke even, for neither one of us had read anything the other had written.

Well, we got along pretty well, both of us, with all these Politicians. In fact I couldent have had a better setting to get acquainted with him. We both took Politicians and their business about equally serious. When the Dinner was over and Mrs. Astor was taking us home—by the way, in a little American touring car—he said he lived near my hotel and would I like to drop by his Apartment?

Well Lady Astor whispered to me, "You go. He don't invite many up there, and don't you miss this."

I said, "Lady, your persuasion is entirely unnecessary. I am there now if he don't change his mind."

Well, I don't mind telling you I went and had the most wonderful evening. For once in my life, I knew enough to keep my mouth shut and just listen. He told me all about his discovery of Maude Adams,[121] and the wonderful association between him and Frohman[122] and Miss Adams for all those years.[123]

I think it's a good idea to split up any of the data that I am gathering for you, and not send too much in one letter, in case the letter is intercepted by Spies or someone that wants to find out something of great importance. So I will do that often. I will send half what I want you to know by one boat and half by the other. It's not probable that one party would capture two of these in succession, not if he knew it. So I will close.

Don't overlook this Mrs. Astor when we are drafting talent from this Country. We havent a single big woman in our Country, politically. We have lots of them but they only reach as far as the County or State line. But she could take those women over there and get their minds on something besides reducing. Her and Baldwin[124] are the best bets in England so far politically.

Your devoted adherant.

W. R.

Special Cable[125]

CALCOOL, *Washhousewhite:*

LONDON, May 18.—Nancy Astor (which is the nom de plume of Lady Astor) is arriving on your side soon. She is the best friend America has here. Please[126] take care of her. She is the only one over here that dont throw rocks at American tourists.

WILLROG.

LONDON, May 18, '26.

My Dear Mr. President: England has the best Statesmen and the Rottenest coffee of any country in the World. I just hate to see morning come, because I have to get up and drink this Coffee. Is there nothing can be done about this? What does Kellogg say? He was over here and had to drink it. Or did Mrs. Kellogg build his for him every morning? I tell you it's the thing that is keeping these Countries apart more than anything I know of. Personally, I will be perfectly willing to sign over my share in the debt settlement for just one good cup of Coffee. Dam it, we give 'em good tea, and all we demand is reciprocity. Look into this, will you? Next to Farmers' relief, it's one of the big problems that is confronting us today. For every Fool American is coming over this summer, and it's the fool vote that we have got to watch for. I would even drink New Orleans Coffee if I had it now.

Best wishes from your Coffee Hound Servant.

W. R.

P. S. How is Pinchot and Pepper[127] making out? I just toured that State and told them that they better look out for this fellow Vare.[128] They all said to me, "Oh, no, Will! The better element are all against him." Well, I knew that, but I also knew Pennsylvania. There are very few of the better element in Pennsylvania. I don't know offhand of a State, according to its population, that has fewer better element. Of course I hope that nothing disastrous turns out,

41

but I warned them three months ago to procure more Better Element.

W. R.

LONDON, May 19, '26.

My Dear Mr. President: At first I was a little discouraged on account of picking Europe to come to this summer. On account of being so many coming here I thought it will not be exclusive enough for me. But you don't know how glad I am now, because almost everybody I know has visited the North Pole this spring. Have you been there yet? The Natives will be offering you a summer White House there, if they haven't already done so. Go if they offer it to you, because I am not refusing anything myself.

The American Club in London, on Piccadilly, wanted to give me a Dinner, and you know what I think of these Dinners. You remember the one you and I attended at the Gridiron Club in Washington. I remember we were both equally bored. It took us till almost one o'clock to eat what little they had, and the speeches outside of yours and mine was terrible; if I remember right, even yours wasent so good. Well, I went here. They are a lot of Americans over here belong to it and they are awful nice fellows, and as soon as the Emigration law is extended, they can come to America.

Pick Cross[129] is the head of the thing, and what America failed to get from England in the way of the debt, why, Pick is taking from them with Vacuum oil.[130] Lord Ashfield[131] was to be there and be one of the speakers to welcome me to England, but he had charge of the Transportation during the strike and couldent keep enough transportation going to get him there. But there was another Lord there that spoke—Lord Dewar.[132] All he is is the man that makes the famous Dewar Whisky.[133] He is given out to be the greatest after-dinner speaker in England.

He gave me a rotten welcome. I couldent tell whether he wanted me to come in or get out. He is great though. I wish we could get him over there. I guess a lot of you wish we could get everything he has over there. But he is a very unique speaker and can conduct himself in almost any company, even if he is a Lord. We had a lot of Sirs there and they let them eat at the first table.

It was a very democratic gathering. Mr. George Grossmith[134] introduced me. He is an English Actor who has been in America long enough to be civilized. He was very good, but I would have ate, or eat, or eaten, whether he had introduced me or not. Say, Joe Coyne[135] was there. You all remember Joe, the American Actor that has been playing in England in Musical Comedies for years. Joe spoke American with a dialect, but I could understand him when he was drinking.

42

Jimmy Gleason,[136] the Author of Is Zat So, was hungry enough to come; and Tom Webster,[137] the greatest Cartoonist in all England. He is the Ding and Ireland[138] of our British Cousins. Mr. Lester Allen,[139] George White's[140] Ace for many years, and Mr. Paul Whiteman and a Gang of his Boys, who are at present playing all over London—they were there. So we made a real American night of it.[141]

Sitting next to me was Mr. Selfridge,[142] the man that owns that Big Department store in London. And say, he is as American as Woolworth.[143] If any American ever goes to London and has a kick about some purchase in Selfridge's Store, why, hunt him up and you will feel like you have met a long lost Uncle. I asked him if he had any trouble with the strike among his help.

"Oh, no, my people don't strike," he said. "I have never had any trouble at all."

Now that is what I was getting at, Mr. President, in a previous letter about these coal men. Why don't they know and understand their men that work for them? Selfridge could make those English mines pay and have the men having Tea with him. Well, it's getting late, so I must close. It's been a late night for one old Country Boy that ain't used to stepping out. You know how it is up in New England when you go home and they keep you up till around 10:30.

Let me know about Pennsylvania and the Farm relief.

Yours devotedly,

W. R.[144]

LONDON, May 19, '26.

My Dear Mr. President: There will be a Song hitting you now if it hassent already hit you. Do what you can to keep people from going entirely cuckoo over it. It is in exchange for Yes, We Have no Bananas, and is called Valencia.[145] It was written for Mistinguette,[146] a singer in a Review in Paris. It ain't the Piece—it's all right—it's the amount of times they will play it. Have Ear muffs ready.

Yours devotedly,

W. R.

HOUSE OF PARLIAMENT, LONDON.[147]

May 20, '26.

Dear Mr. President:

Papers have just reached me telling of the good fortune that has befallen the voters of Illinois and Pennsylvania[148] and the jealousy that it aroused in the other cheaper states.

While things were kinder quiet over in Cuckooland and as I was not a resident voter in Illinois, or Pennsylvania, and, had no chance to clean up, or get in on any of the heavy jack, why, of course, there was no use in my hanging around over there.

Personally, I am in favor of money being spent on elections. The more money the better. If they can get contributions from rich men and distribute them around among the poor and needy I think it's a good thing. It puts money into circulation that otherwise would be loaned to Europe at a "ruinous rate of Interest" (which is 1 per cent.).

A voter nowadays has very little chance of getting anything from his Senator after election, and why shouldent he get what he can before? Besides, the fellow may not get elected, and in that case the vote they sold did no harm and dident break the fellow that made the contributions. So my slogan is "Bigger and higher-priced elections."

Mayby that's what has been the matter with our Government in Washington. Everybody seems unanimous that something is the matter. Well, mayby it has been too cheap; I am a great believer in high-priced people. If a thing cost a lot it may not be any better, but it adds a certain amount of class that the cheap thing can never approach; in the long run its the higher-priced things that are the cheapest.

You let a Senator go in there with some million-dollar contributions behind him and you can't tell me that he wouldent command some respect, and that is what we have got to get back in our Senate that has been lost—respect. No one has any real respect for it any more; its just a Club that ninety-six men belong to, and pay no dues.

Now you can't run that cheap a Club and make it pay; I tell you the day has past in America when the successful Candidate can go about bragging on the fact that he "was elected on $22.45 worth of 5-cent Cigars." We don't want that type of man; if he is not a big enough man to hand out over a nickle Cigar he is not a big enough man to run the biggest business in the World. Besides we don't want men in there who would represent voters that smoked 5-cent Cigars. No man is any better than his constituency, and if Nickle voters elected him he is a nickle man at heart. That's exactly what's the matter with the Senate now, we have too many nickle Senators in there.

This is the day of big business and quick turnover, you can't do anything on a shoe-string any more. It takes heavy dough to do anything nowadays. If a man hasent made a success out of his own business we don't want him in practicing on ours. The cheap man is the high-priced man in the finish, its not what you pay a man to go in, its what he has cost you after he gets in that we have to look out for.

We got a lot of Senators in there that have been elected on nothing but a Slogan, but what have they cost us after they got in?

You see it ain't the initial cost of a Senator that we have to look out for, its his upkeep after we get him in there. He may be the deciding vote on one appropriation bill that will cost the country more than a hundred high-priced men would. You take a fellow that has never juggled with real jack and he don't know the value of it, a billion and a million sound so much alike that he thinks all the difference is just in the spelling.

You see with a cheap Guy in there the voters never got a penny out of the election, and nobody gets anything, so I am a strong advocate for selling the seats to the highest bidder, they do it on the Stock exchange and it has proven successful, and I don't see why we can't do it with the Senate seats.

You see the men that layed out our Constitution in the first place looked far enough ahead to see, in fact they must have had a premonition that at some time in the distant future there would be a bunch of men in there that dident know any more about Government than me or Nick Altrock[149] knows about Einsteins' theory.[150] Well, these old fellows in those days just slipped some things in that Constitution to cover these very times, in fact they almost made it fool proof, so due to their foresightedness no one we put in can do us a whole lot of damage.

In other words, when you come right down to it the importance of a Senate job is mighty overrated. They can only do us little temporary damages, so it really don't matter much who is in there. So lets fix it so the thing pays somebody and I am for it paying the common man, and where can you get any commoner man than a voter? So lets raise the ante on the amount any man can contribute to another man's Campaign, take the lid off and make the sky the limit. Let 'em go out and spend all they can. In the past what has the voter got, nothing but a button and a torch.

Let's make elections something to look forward to, not something to dread. The Constitution of the United States gives the right of every free man to get all he can for whatever he has. That Constitution set no price on anything, it wisely allowed every person freedom, and bargaining power, so what has the ordinary working man got? Nothing but his vote, but Washington and Jefferson and Uncle Joe Cannon and Chauncey Depew[151] and men of that time knew too much to put a limit on what he was allowed to get for what he possessed, so a later Government limits the amount to be paid for rights of American Citizens, and I bet you if you took it to the Supreme Court and you could get all of them to stay awake long enough four of them would vote one way and three the other (that's the nearest they would ever come to agreeing on anything).

45

When you regulate the price that a man can spend for votes you are flirting with the very backbone of American Liberty. You can tell me what I can't drink, and you can tell me how I have to have my hair cut, and how long my bed sheets must be, but by the spirit of Abraham Lincoln you can't tell me how much I can sell my vote for. It's mine and it's all a free country has given me for nothing, and I am going to hold out to do with it what I please. If I want to sell it I will sell it, if I want to keep it and not use it at all, that is my inestimable right by the Constitution. If I want to even give it away the only thing I have to look out for is the Insane Asylum.

You have monkeyed too much already with our Liberty, but this is the last straw. I want to see the day come when the least a vote will sell for is a Ford Car, and not a Henry Clay Cigar. If we can't be a good nation let's at least not be accused of being a cheap Nation. Besides who cares nowadays who is elected to anything, they are not in office three days till we realize our mistake and wish the other one had got in?

We are a Nation that runs in spite of and not on account of our Government. If you do as I say we can make election day just as happy as Christmas Day, and twice as profitable, high-priced votes means prosperity to everybody.

Now I hope Mr. Coolidge that this plan will meet with your entire approval, and if you have the welfare of the voters at heart and not the Politicians, why I know it will. I would submit the plan to the Democrats but they havent got enough money to carry it through. Yours for the welfare of the Commonwealth.

Your confidential arranger in Europe,

WILL.

LONDON, May 20, '26.

My Dear Mr. President: I was setting around the Hotel this afternoon after the Dinner at the American Club, and there comes a ring at the Phone and my Boy Bill Jr., who is with me, answered the Phone, and he says, "Dad, there is somebody wants to talk to you."

I says, " Find out who it is."

He says, "It is General Trotter,[152] the Equerry to the Prince of Wales."[153]

He is an awful nice fellow. He was over in America with the Prince and everybody liked him.

He said, "The Prince would like to see you. Can you come on over?" I told him I thought it could be arranged. Where does he live? He says, "York House. Come on over."[154]

Say, listen I got there, drove in a kind of a Court Yard. A Soldier was marching around. But, Lord, in England one Soldier marching in

46

front of a place don't mean anything. Why, in the House of Parliament, with absolutely nothing in the future depending on it, there must have been a thousand I had to pass before I could get in even to their Gallery. While here was the absolute Kid himself with just one[155] prowling around out there in the yard.

I said, "Where does the Prince live?" He nodded to a door. I went there and rung a bell and along came a Butler, or what I had come to know as a Butler—no livery or uniform. Now here is what I want you to get—he was the only Servant I saw in this whole layout. He called General Trotter, and we went through a kind of a room and then on upstairs and through one more room. They were big but nothing particularly great to them. It looked about like an Oil Millionaire's home in Oklahoma, only more simple and in better taste. And Long Island Homes? His whole place would have got lost in their what they humorously call their Main Saloon.

We were approaching a closed door, when suddenly it opened and here was the Prince. He shook hands like a Rotary Club President that has been coached in the best way to make friends.

Now before we go any further, "How was he dressed?" asked half-naked America. I know the Boys all want to know, and the Girls are just crazy to hear. He had on a very plain brown checked suit. The only distinguishing feature I could see between this and most other brown-suit wearers who try to imitate him was that his suit fitted. He is rather small and slender, but very well built. Had on tan shoes and a soft collar and four-in-hand tie, and it was about 3:30 in the afternoon. So now Young America will know what to wear at 3:30 in the afternoon. Come to think about it, it was the same suit I had seen him wear over at the House of Commons every day during the session. So it gave me and my one suit real encouragement.

He looked a lot better than when over in America; that is, more rested and fit. You know we like to run him ragged. I have always doubted if Dempsey could have stood that trip the Prince made over there.

He says, "I hear you are a Journalist now. This is no interview, remember; just renewing old acquaintanceship."

Well, that was about the first compliment I had had, that being a Journalist part, and I told him that I was mighty glad he had remembered me; that I dident know but what he might be looking on his tour to America in the nature of a slumming Expedition, or, in other words, a Night Out, and like anyone you meet on a night out, you don't want to see them in the morning. But he said he certainly dident want it to be that way with him, and he had already proved it by asking me over.

I told him this would not be any interview; that I would not ask him the usual questions; "How did you like America?" and "When are you to be married, and to whom?" I told him anything you say to me is just ad lib, and nobody will ever know it but President Coolidge and America.

One thing that I want you to know that will establish his Character better than anything else and show you that he has a real sense of humor is when I first come in I said, "Hello, old-timer! How are you falling these days?" and he replied as quick as a flash, "All over the place. I got my shoulder broke since I saw you last."[156]

I said, "We will have to get you better Jumping horses that don't fall."

He started in right away defending the horses he had ridden: "Oh, they were very splendid Horses; they were just unfortunate in falling, that's all."

He right away asked about you, Mr. Coolidge, and how you were, and remembered with very much satisfaction his visit to you in Washington. I complimented him on the way his Country had handled the great strike which had just ended and told him that I wouldent have missed it for anything, for I thought it had been a great boost for the British Empire in remaining so cool.[157] I spoke of how quick the Empire had mobilized their forces.

He said, "Well, it was not unexpected, you know. We were all prepared."

I told him I thought the Government papers had rather over-emphasized the calling of it as a Revolution, because that is what they had spoken of it as. He said no, he dident think so; that had it been a success, there was no doubt Leaders among them would have tried to have gone much further than just a raise in wages.

Now that shows he had a pretty good line on just what was going on. Anybody that thinks he don't know about anything but when does the next dance start is crazy.[158] I asked him if he had his Ranch in Canada yet, and he says, "You bet your life I have it. Canada is a great Country." I then told him that I had just played in Toronto a couple of weeks before and that they were having quite a time there over the tariff on Automobiles from America. He knew all about it, how much it was, and said he hoped that they would do nothing that would kill off their own Industry, as they were just getting a good start.

We then talked about an old rancher out adjoining him. Old Man Lane[159] who had died. He paid him a beautiful tribute and spoke about what a fine old fellow he was, and we exchanged stories about the old fellow, for I had known him for years, and he was a unique Character. I asked him about my friend Guy Weadick,[160] who ranches near him. He said Guy had put him on a fine Wild West Show when up there last. We just talked like a couple of old Hill Billies about neighbors and friends, and I don't think that he will consider this any breach of confidence by me reporting it to you. I told him that I was surprised to find him at this York House; that I thought he lived at some other place.

He said, "No, I have lived here now for several years."

I asked him, "But dident some of your folks[161] leave you some other place?"

He laughed and said, "Yes, Marlborough House; but it's not ready yet."

I said, "Ready? What's the idea? Haven't they moved a bed in there yet, or are you waiting for a cookstove? A Canadian Rancher ought not to kick on being shy a few luxuries, like a bed or Grub, or matches or something like that." I said, "This ain't a bad Joint you have here."

"No, we have plenty of room," he admitted.

All this time I was looking around the room. It was just a very ordinary living room, with a fireplace burning, and a table with a lot of books on it and a mantelpiece with Pictures that looked like he and his Brothers and Princess Mary[162] at different ages of their lives, and a big Picture of his Mother in just an ordinary little frame in the Center of the mantel. None of these were paintings or great big things; they were just ordinary Photographs. Some of them looked like they had been enlargements from snapshots. The Table had books. One of them that I noticed was The life of Queen Victoria.[163]

It seemed to be some new one and had a wrapper on it. There was a Statue of a Horse with a saddle on it. I went over to ask about it. He said it was not a Polo Pony, but a tired Hunter.

The whole room just gave you the feeling of some boy's room off to school, or some boy that was fortunate enough to have his own room at home and fixed it the way he wanted.

I never felt any more at home in a place in my life. Although I dident have any room just exactly like this in my house, I did have a fireplace, and a mantel with Pictures. Not royalty perhaps, but to me they were. Of course we had to talk some Polo. He said Lacy and Miles[164] were there in England from the Argentine.

We talked of Captain Melville and Lord Weatherford, who were in Florida last winter. He then asked me of some fellow I dident know who he had heard had just had a bad fall in a hunt near Baltimore; said he had just sent him a cable. Shows you he don't overlook much friendship stuff, to think of some fellow who got a fall away over in Baltimore. I would have figured it served him right for being in Baltimore.[165]

I asked him if he was staying long in England. He said yes, he had even taken quarters here. I told him I was getting out of here to go down and see Mussolini. That led to talk about Mussolini. He said he had never met him.[166] He said he must be a very remarkable man. I told him if all I hear is true about him[167] he must be a bear. Said he would like to see him.

He liked the Argentine and all South America.[168] He even got out his maps and showed me where he had gone there. Told me and showed me how he got snowbound for I think it was a week, trying to get over to Chili. We talked about the good horses they have there. Then about Africa.[169]

Then he had to pull it of course. He asked about how was Prohibition getting along over home. Well, I told him he saw how it was getting along when he was over there. He asked me about the Pony I had bought of his, for Mr. Ziegfeld's little Girl—with Ziegfeld's money.[170] He tried even to remember its name, I couldent help him out any. I could remember the price, $2100, but from then on I couldent remember anything. He said he was looking forward to another visit with us some time.

I told him, "Well, boy, the old latch-string will sho be hanging out for you anywhere you want to light in America. If at any time you feel that you are not appreciated over here, why, come on over." I told him you, Mr. President, would give him a room in one end of the White House. He could be a kind of a Social accomplice to you. Just think of the things you could get out of by sending him. So I hope I dident take in too much ground by offering the old spare room, because he is a great Kid, not because he remembered me.[171] But I felt that in remembering me he had remembered ordinary America.

Well, I had been there for over an hour. I don't know how long I was supposed to stay, and I don't care. This is not an interview, and it's not supposed to be one. I dident ask him any questions. I just visited with him. He had a good word for everybody and everything. When he spoke seriously of the strike he spoke of how square the men that struck had been and the gentlemanly way they had handled themselves, and he was proud that even I would think that the whole thing had acted to the credit of Great Britain.

Now that just gives you a little slant on why those people are cuckoo about him. Those pictures all around there of his own folks sorter made a hit with me. No, I dident see a single Girl's Picture outside of Princess Mary's. So there will be no wedding this year.[172]

Just before I left I told him about seeing him a few days before and how I sat not far behind him in the House of Parliament, and that I wanted to climb over and say hello, but that I was afraid they might revive the old chopping block out at the Tower of London if anyone annoyed a Prince.

He laughed and said, "I should like to see you under that block and hear what you had to say then."

There's a fine friend to have, somebody that wants your head to be severed just to see what you would say. So I better be thinking up something pretty good, for when that Guy gets to be King he is liable to get a laugh at the expense of my neck. But just between you and I, Calvin, he don't care any more about being King than you would going back to Vice President again. But he would be a great old King.

Well, I must stop. That's all I have to report tonight. He is about all I saw today. Well, he is enough for one day.

Yours devotedly,

W. R.

Special Cable[173]

CALCOOL, *Whitehousewash:*

LONDON, May 20.—American tourists are still coming by the thousands and bragging about where they come from. Sometimes you think France really has been too lenient with them.

Yours for quieter visitors,

WILLROG.

House of Lords, London,[174]

May 21, '26.

Dear Mr. Coolidge:

Well all I know is just what I read in the papers. I am so far away that you will find my information kinder dull reading. Do you know that a murder is two weeks old before I get an inkling of it over here? I don't hear a bit of late interesting news like that till the party has mayby had time to shoot two or three more or have their trial and be out on bond. Funny thing, these papers over here don't go in for murder much. They certainly are old fashioned about what is news. A fellow in Chicago can go out and do a fair day's shooting and maybe come in with six or eight notches in the cork of his hootch flask, and they won't cable a word of it. The way they do the news of crime and robberies from America, they just run them in a regular little place down in the corner of the paper under the heading:

51

AMERICAN PROSPERITY

Yesterday's Market Report:

Killed (by Automobile) 32. Killed (by Gunshot ond Other Natural Causes) 21

Robberies 824

They won't tell you who was killed, who was robbed, who did the robbing, or any of the details. You can't find out if you had a friend done any good or not. They run it just like a baseball box score. You get the results and that's all. Now you see they couldn't run a paper five minutes like that over home. Then here is another funny thing about them over here. If they happen to have a murder here (they had one last year), why they don't show any pictures of it at all. If they have any pictures of the fellow who did the killing, why they just let the police use them. They seem to think the police will do more toward catching him than the readers can, and the funny part about it is that they do. Well, can you imagine a fellow leading a Gang over home, and going in to rob a place and shooting a half dozen, getting away, and then not having a single paper publish a dozen pictures of him? Say he would be so sore he would call on that Editor and tell him something. He just about would be so sore that he wouldn't rob any more. And imagine if they didn't publish his Girl's picture, under the heading "Master Mind behind Gang Leader." You keep her picture out of the paper and you will see how long she will continue this "master minding." Over here they don't care if he had a Girl. He could have a Harem if he wanted to; nobody would ever read about it. After the murder is over the next thing you read about him is: "He was cheerful to the last and ate a hearty breakfast." If he wants to do any Heroing here he better do it before he commits any crime. For from that time on the papers are going to cease to be his Press Agents.

Do you know, as a real matter of fact, that Criminal Statistics of England prove that in all the Murders that have been committed here, that over 50 per cent of the ones that committed the crime have committed suicide before or right after being caught? They do that rather than face the law. They know that they will be caught, and they know what will happen to them after they are caught. So rather than face it they kill themselves. Can you imagine a fellow in some big City over home committing suicide for fear he would be caught, or funnier still one committing suicide for fear of what would happen to him after he did get caught? It wouldn't be possible for an American criminal to commit suicide. It would require too big a sense of humor.

They got the quaintest ideas over here of right and wrong. Lots of the Cafes are not allowed to serve anything to drink after twelve o'clock. But they have Cabaret shows that runs to two or three o'clock, and after twelve there is not a drop to drink on any table, and no one has a bottle hid under the table, and not a flask in the house. They seem to think because it's a law they have to obey it. They got the funniest ideas that way. They seem to think the whole thing is on the level. All in the world you have to do over here to a get a fellow not to do anything is just to let him know that it is against the law. Now these papers over here will print something about the League of Nations, or France's Financial Trouble, or Mexico, or Our Congress even, before they will print crime stuff. I don't see how in the world they make a living with them. And the Policemen, especially the Traffic ones, when they catch you, they are so nice about it that they don't seem like traffic Policemen at all. You never hear one say "Ha, Bo! Pull over there! Say, where do you think you are going? What's the big idea? You the only one on the road?" They are so nice about it here that it is almost a pleasure to have stopped and made their acquaintance.

But, as I say, they are just so far behind the times over here they don't know any better. They think they are progressing. So that's what makes it so hard to get any news out of their papers that would be of any interest to you all over there.

I am leaving here soon and going up to Scotland to see Barney Baruch[175] at his Grouse Castle. They have killed about all the gentle Grouse up there now, and they are just waiting till the Scotchmen get some more gentled for them. Barney and I got to sorter lay out our lines for the old 1928 handicap. I hate to mix Politics and Grouse and Bagpipes and Kilts, but '28 looks like a Democratic year. It's two years away. That's the main reason it looks like a Democratic year. Any two years away always looks like a Democratic year. In fact any two years away is a Democratic year. Democratic Politics is what you might call future Politics. But Barney and I have a pretty good layout of a Campaign. He is going to furnish the Candidate, and I am going to furnish the Platform. We have really never had a well written platform. It's always had ink splotches on it, or beer stains or something. So I have an idea of an entirely new one, that will give us everything but the votes. Now, we got to look to you Mr. Coolidge for the votes. The way you and the weather act between now and the fall of '28 will decide the votes for us. Democratic Candidates have been nominated in the back rooms of hotels for years. But this is the first time one ever was chosen out on the moors of Old Scotland, while we are waiting for the Scotchmen to drive some half-breed Prairie Chickens by.

So the next President, if he is elected on the Democratic Party, out of respect to our judgment we will insist that he wear Kilts, and have a Scotch Economy platform.

Now, I know I shouldent touch on crime or any of those little things. It's the big things I am sent to look after, but you wont mind my engaging in trivialities once in a while.

Your European "Cottage,"
WILL.

Naples, Italy, May 25, '26.

My Dear President:

You ought to see the tourists here. When you havent seen anything in your own Country, have never been further away from home than the barn, why those are the people who go see Italy. It's to the Tourists what Hollywood is to the visiting Iowans. Start in with Naples for that is about as low down as you can get, without going to Sicily.

Pompaei,[176] that was at one time the Beverley Hills of Italy, was caught in a landslide. It covered the city with a second mortgage. Now if you like buried cities you cant beat this one, personally I dont care for buried cities, I find enough of them on my tour over home instead of going clear to europe to seek one. But it is a very good example of early buried architecture. Every Tourist is "so surprised" to find the houses and rooms "Just as they were before" Vesuvius ash tray run over. I don't know why they should be "so surprised." How was it going to change after they were all snowed under. There has been some Scandal unearthed as well as Art. It seems Some of the "Boys about Town" dident reach the right house before the visitation of providence. You should see Pompaei. Philadelphia comes nearer approaching it than any big City I know of.

I must tell you about Naples, that's the railroad stop for Pompaei. But on our right as we go back there is a mountain, or a high hill rather, looks like somebody had plowed up the top of it. Well that's Vesuvius. Vesuvius is kinder known in history as being a sort of local Police or enforcement mountain, when some City got to putting it on a little too strong in the way of Night life, why Vesuvius makes a raid on them and it is generally so complete that their mode of living is entirely remodeled. That's why I am going to move out of Hollywood and Beverly Hills. It just seems an act of providence, that there is a mountain right back of them about the size of Vesuvius. Now I am not saying this to knock Real Estate values there. Paris, France, and Claremore Oklahoma, had the right idea; they built out on the flat not near any Mountain. You can get away with anything in those two places, without fear of a moral landslide.

Did you ever see the bay of Naples that you have heard and read so much about? Did you ever see the harbor in San Francisco? Well it makes the bay of Naples look like the Chicago drainage Canal, and I am from Los Angeles Too. Why even the harbor of Los Angeles with its growing barley fields, and its thriving Subdivisions, if it had any water in it would be better than Naples. Why Houston stole a better harbor from Galveston than Naples is. It hasent got the blue water that Naples has but it will float an old tug full of cotton. Why Miami Florida if they ever cleaned those gin bottles out of that Harbor of theirs would lay it all over the Mediteranian. The whole Mediteranian is overestimated as a fluid for cruising purposes. It's green and Blue and all that and has beautiful colors, but it hasent got the stamina or the body to it to hold up boats like the Leviathan, or the Majestic,[177] or even the Mayflower. Mind you if you have a passion for bays why go there, but Tampa or San Diego can bay all around anything they got in the way of bays.

The greatest gag over here anywhere is the Goats they have driving around the streets in place of milk wagons. If you want milk and you hear the goats going up your alley with their bells ringing why you dont hang out a sign, you just stick your head out and "bleat" like a goat. The number of bleats will designate the amount of tin cups full you get. I am the last one in the world to see anything and not see some good in it. There is no chance of watered stock, the Milk you get may not be the particular kind of milk that you would like to have but its what you ordered, and thats more than you can say at home. Its Goat's milk, its the pure extract of the Angora, no pump connection anywhere. You drink Goats milk steady for two weeks and you can butt your way into a Bronx local. Three months steady on it, and you have cloven hoofs and an odor. That's why so many Singers and Tenors come from Italy. There is no voice advancement in Cow Juice. It's the shrill bleat of the Nanny that brings out all that is worst in a Tenor. If you cant afford to go to Italy to study why just get a Goat and develop your Soprano at home.

Yours devotedly,

WILL.

ROME, June 1, '26.
[This is Rome, Italy, not Georgia.]
THE PRESIDENT OF THEM UNITED STATES,

My Dear Mr. President: Well, I come clear to Italy, as you know,

Boss, just to see Mussolini, and see for you if his style of Government was as bad as the Republicans over home. He is the busiest man in the world today and I dident know if I would be able to see him personally and privately or not. As I told you before, I had letters from everybody but you. But after all it has to be arranged through our ambassador, Mr. Fletcher.

Well, Nick and Alice had done nobly by me with Fletcher. They gave me a real personal letter, and in addition the day I landed in Rome they sent him a long Cablegram telling him to be sure and have the Duce see me. Now that was mighty fine of them, and it's just little thoughtful things like that that Alice and Nick are doing that is going to make him awful hard to forget some November. Mind you, I am not criticizing you. But if Senator Borah could be thoughtful enough, and take time enough from his busy life to give me one, why, there was absolutely no excuse for you.

Well, this Fletcher is a bear. He is a real go-get-'em Kid. He fought with the Rough-riders in Cuba with the original Mussolini, and has been representing us all over the country for 24 years. I had lunch with them at his flat—they have a painting there—the day he celebrated his exact 24th year. Mr. Kellogg had sent him a nice Telegram, which by the way was mighty thoughtful of Mr. Kellogg. He is a good man for us to watch, this Fletcher, if anything better shows up. But don't know how anything better could show up that would beat Rome.

Well, he got busy right away, and he arranged a date for me for Friday at twelve o'clock. Now that was about 6 days away, and it seems that Mussolini was going to Genoa to speak in the meantime. You know, over there they have no Radio's and you have to go and tell them personally. He can't lay in bed and talk to everybody that hasent static, like you can.

Well, he got back from Genoa all right, as they had disarmed every Irishwoman of even their snuff. Well, the more I was there in Italy, and the more I would hear about him, and the more I would see what he had done, why, the bigger he got to me. As the date grew nearer, I commenced getting kinder scared. Everybody in the world had either flew to the north Pole this summer or was trying to see Mussolini. Well, I took the Mussolini end, because there are two Poles but only one Mussolini.

Now in the meantime I read up on him and talked to everybody that could talk sense—American—and I tried and did find the high light in his rise to this tremendous success. Everybody in Italy told me what shape the Country was in before, and they all also related to me the fight he had to get in to straighten the Country out,

56

and in relating it they would all mention what everyone of them admitted was the turning point in his Party's favor.

Now as you know, Mr. President, you sent me here especially to see and study this man's Methods. He was my objective when I left home. You wanted me to see and write you from the Human Interest point. So I will have to first tell you of his weapon. It did more to put him where he is today than any other one thing in the world. In speaking of it here to you I know that I am within the bounds of propriety, because it is so well known and spoken of everywhere in Italy, and I will also quote you exactly from Articles which were written by the great English writer Sir Percival Phillips,[178] K.B.E., and were published in the London Daily Mail, and afterwards in book form. I will quote exact from his Book:

"In the war, Fascisti fought against Bolshevism. Fascisti—the Black Shirts—used many weapons. By far the most effective of these was Castor Oil. The Fascisti were constantly encountering acts of disloyalty which deserved punishment on a lower scale. So they conceived the idea of purging Society in this simple way. Some were too old to be beaten or thrown into Jail, some too young. But all ages received some of it if they did acts against their Government, or the Fascisti. He was given a couple of large tumblerfuls, and if he dident drink it voluntarily, his nose was held and he had to swallow. Thereafter castor oil became the sovereign remedy for Red Madness. It was given to all breeds of Bolsheviks from Desperado's from the criminal classes to the Intellectual's who were always preaching to overthrow the Government. The effect was unfailing. I am told that a patient never rendered himself liable to a second dose when he returned from his retirement, pale and haggard.

"He found himself an object of ridicule instead of a martyr. Fascisti would pass him by with an ironic inquiry as to the state of his health, and even his own Bolsheviki friends had difficulty in expressing sympathy without showing amusement. Ridicule then became a powerful ally of the Black Shirts. The psychologists at the head of the movement—which was Mussolini—gauged exactly the mentality of their opponents and when less subtle Leaders have relied mistakenly on brute Force alone, the Fascisti waged war with fine discrimination. So formidable has castor oil become that it is now the formidable argument for suppressing even disorder. Adria, in Venetia, gives it for drunkenness. Not only is the drunkard to be given it but the man who sold it to him, or if sold to boys under 16 years of age, and a bottle of castor oil is to be kept in every café just as a warning. Through the entire Fascisti penal system there runs this same sardonic humor, a warning is generally necessary."

Now those are the bare facts as they were known and were published everywhere. "The Life of Mussolini," by Marpherita Sarfatti,[179] the most complete book of any man's life ever published, treats in a like manner, of this modern remedy. The reason I tell you all this is so you won't think that it is some concoction of mine to derive humor from a very serious situation in the History of a great country. It took Statesmen and men of foresight to do a brainy thing like that. In all my reading or observing of the workings of a remedy against political plottings and minor crimes, this is, I think, the absolute masterpiece of History. Not only from the humorous but from the efficient standpoint, I know of nothing that would lessen a man's political aspirations more than this. Just think of the possibilities not only in Italy, but in our country.

How many dozens of things can you think of offhand that it would improve, over our present remedies, and then the hundreds of things that should be remedied that has no particular law applied to them now, at all, but that this would fix. So this gave me a real line and a real issue to work on when I saw him. In other words, it gave me courage, for I knew the man must have humor.

Well, the day arrived and I said to myself, I am going in a-grinning, even if they decide to revive the old Roman Colliseum, and put me in there and give me just three jumps in front of a Lion. I had heard that Mussolini sits in the far-back corner of a great room, and that in this long walk up to him from the door he has your number before you hit the quarter pole. Well, the only unemployment I saw in the whole of Italy was the people that was waiting in these rooms to see Mussolini; I thought, my goodness, I will never get in here.

I was accompanied by Mr. Warren Robbins[180] the next in charge under Mr. Fletcher at the Embassy. He was my Host and Interpreter. Mussolini's office is a big Palace in the center of Rome. Right on the dot, at twelve o'clock, somebody said something to Robbins in Italian, and I was headed for the most talked of, the most discussed—the man that has done more for one race of people in three years than any man living ever did; a Napoleon, but with peace; the man that I had never even in any of his pictures seen smiling. This man, with all this on his mind, I was going in to see if I could get a laugh out of him, or find out what kind of a Duck he was. My friend, Marcosson, I knew, had just got a wonderful interview from him, but his was along Government, or economical and commonsense lines; but I didn't know what I was going to be able to lead him into.

I had asked people, but no one had ever had the nerve to try him out on anything less than a world problem. I knew that everybody that faced him for the first time always were kinder scared, or leary of him. And I also knew that a big man gets tired being just done nothing to but be complimented. So I says, "Benito"—that's his Christian name, and in Spanish means pretty. That is the only false alarm I found him sailing under. He was not what I would term pretty. He was cute, but not pretty. Well, I says, "Come on, Claremore, les see what Rome has got. I am going to treat this fellow like he was nobody but Hiram Johnson.[181] Get your Lions ready for a foot race, in case I dissplease."

Now in the first place I wasent dressed like I should have been. Warren and everybody else that I saw had on what they called a Morning Coat. It has the long tail, but neither the coat, nor the pants, nor the vest, has to match. In fact they are not allowed to match; if they do they are wrong. Well, my suit all matched; that's all it did do. I could see Warren looking me over, but he dident say anything. He just figured: "Well, he will perhaps be thrown out anyway, so let it go." Well they had the distance right to his desk. It's just about as far as from the middle of the stage to the wings if your last joke has died on you.

Well, I come in a-grinning. I thought he has got to be a pretty tough Guy if he don't grin with you. Well, he did, and he got up and come out and met us at about the 4th green, shook hands smiling, and asked in English, "Interview?" I said "No Interview." Well, that certainly did make the hit with him; he was standing facing me, and he put both hands on my shoulders and said, "Hurray. Bravo. No Interview."

I guess he has got so tired of people asking him a lot of the same set questions and then, perhaps, seeing them missquoted afterwards. I said to him, I come clear from America not to see how your country was run. If it's run wrong, it's nothing to me. From all the pictures and all we know about you, you are looking like Napoleon, and I come to see is Mussolini a Regular Guy. Well, he got that in English, and it seemed to please him, and he seemed to start right in to prove to me that he was one. He understands most everything you say to him in English—that is, he seems to understand most of it. Personally, I believe he gets more of it than he lets on, and he always answered me back in English, if it was just some short reply; but if he had to explain or it was a long sentence, why he would tell it to Warren, and they talked in French, because Warren spoke that language better; it don't make much difference to Mussolini, outside of English, he is a bear on any of the others .

He asked me if I spoke French. That was his first comedy line. Can you imagine me speaking French? I bet, though, I could start

59

in and learn it as quick as I could English, at that. I then asked, "You hold a lot of different jobs here—you know, he is the Mcadoo[182] of Italy for running everything—you are Minister of—" He interrupted me, and laughingly counted off on his fingers, "Me—one, two, three, four, five, six—Me, Six Ministers," and laughed as he told me. He had sense of humor enough to realize what an outsider would think of one man holding six so-prominent positions. But he also had the good sense to know that he was the only one could hold them right now.

I asked him, How much do you get for being all these and running this whole shooting match like you do. He understood without interpreter, and said, "Oh, not so much," and did his fingers together, as one does when they insinuate money. And as a matter of fact he only gets one thousand dollars a year in our money. I shouldent tell you this, Mr. Coolidge, but I want you to know what other men are doing for one 75th, and don't even mention "economy." I then told him the reason I asked was that I was prepared to make him a better offer, that I would give him more for being one Minister, or Cabinet member, over home than he got for all six over here. He laughed. I couldent tell whether he took it as a compliment or a knock. I then told him that while he was doing all this Minister business that France would perhaps engage him, that Briand[183] was only in for weekends; he said, "No France Minister; no permanent position in France." That showed he had quite a smathering of humor and also a good business eye for a permanent job.

Like every man you talk too, he likes to ask the questions sometimes. He then asked me in a very confidential way and in very good English—because I bet he asks this to everybody—"W-h-a-t h-a-s i-m-p-r-e-s-s-e-d y-o-u m-o-r-e i-n I-t-a-l-y." Well I knew that everybody had always told him that it was the "Marvelous development that had taken place in the last three years." But I told him that it was two things—he seemed very interested—one was the amount of Automobiles meeting and neither one ever knowing which side the other was going to pass him on, and yet nobody ever got hit, and the other thing was the amount of Bicycles ridden, and I never saw anyone ever fixing a puncture.

Well this answer kinder set him back for a minute. I could tell the way he acted that he had got it, even without Warren interpreting it to him. He laughed, but you could tell he was dissappointed. I was the only one that had not noticed the "marvelous improvement in the last three years." But he was humorous and game and he come right back with, "yes, we have very good Bicycle tires here in Italy." This last reply of his was through Mr. Warren. You know, here is a thing about foreigners. If they know they don't speak a thing well, they don't say it in that language, they are afraid of us laughing or inwardly criticizing their pronunciation. But it's just the opposite with an American, you give him three words all said wrong in some language and he will go out of his way to use them. There is no humiliation on his part. He is proud if he only gets one letter right in the whole word.

Now there was times during the conversation when he wasent watching and he would answer regardless of how he spoke it. I then asked him right out if he was the originator of the castor-oil treatment. He laughed and winked and said, "Very good, eh?" He dident say outright that it was his idea, but he winked as he said, "Very good, eh?" and he seemed to be rather proud of the idea, and I don't blame him, because it was the greatest idea put into execution in the entire History, and we can't go back of results. It was the turning point in Italy's fight against the Bolsheviki, and all the results that I will later enumerate that have been so wonderful in the progress of modern Italy were absolutely traceable to this key remedy, castor oil. Why not talk about it if it saved an Empire.

He then said, through Mr. Warren, "No castor oil in two years. When we were fighting and trying to save the country against the Bolsheviks, we used to find them and"—then he dropped back into English—"one fellow, he not so bad, we give him half leiter, next fellow, he bad boy, we give him ONE leiter," and he laughed and sure got a kick out of telling this. A leiter is somewhere less or in close proximity to what, in sense, is a quart.

Well, then I got to what I was leading up too; as he couldent go to America, I asked him would he sell me the recipe for this castor oil over there, that I wanted to give the Senate of the United States some of it, and the Congressmen, on account of being "not so bad," just about half a leiter. He laughed at that, for he had read of them; but the next line was the one that got the real guffaw out of him. I said I was going to Russia, and he interrupted me. "Oh, Russia, See, See! You take recipe to Russia, very good for Russia, castor oil. I give you free." I wanted to suggest it for Charley Dawes to administer to the Senate during a filibuster. It would solve his problem. Well, we had some good laughs over the possible problems that the remedy might be administered for, including Democratic Conventions. I know of nothing that would lessen a political ambition any more, and while he was going good I thought I will ask him a few questions right quick while he is not noticing, and I can tell imediately how he stands on them by the way he looks. I told him I had just been in Geneva, and attended the Preliminary Dissarmament Conference, and what did he think about Dissarmament?

He again laughed, and winked at me as good as to say, "Why do you want to make me laugh." Then he replied, "No dissarmament; we dissarm when England dissarm on sea; when France in Air and land. So you see we never have to dissarm." Say there is the smartest thing I have heard in Europe, said in a few words. Poor old America, when they can't think of anything else to talk about they scare up Dissarmament. He then pulled another very funny line about this meeting which was on in Geneva, and which was just what they were doing. He said "They appoint committee; committee appoint committee; this committee appoint committee to appoint another committee, round and round, like dog biting at own tail." He said a saucer full right then.

I then asked him the question that is uppermost in everybody's mind, here and abroad: What's going to happen to all this, if something happens to you? Now that is not very nice to be asking a fellow that is supposed to be in delicate health. It's kinder like asking a sick person, "Have you made any arrangements about who shall preside at your funeral?" I thought well he has been so very accomidating up to now, that I just as well do something to displease him and see how he is when riled up. But he stuck out his chest and let me feel of his arm, and he said, "Mussolini feel pretty good yet."

You know, I have, and of course you have heard about this terrible stomach trouble he is supposed to have. And then, I have, on just as good authority, heard it denied. We often speak of a man's stomach in regard to his amount of nerve. Well, if that's any sign of a stomach I would like to trade him mine for his, and there has never been nothing the matter with mine outside of nerve. If it's a bad stomach that is doing all this in Italy, why, what the world needs right now is more bad stomachs. Even just a little billiousness would help France.

I then asked him who would carry on the work when he was no more. I wasent, as you see, exactly in there to show any particular tact or diplomacy. I was after some news and I dident care what blunders I committed to get it. He them told me, "I have this all going so good now that it could be run by anyone, or by several different men. It has shown that it will work and is the best thing, so why should anyone want to change it. It's not the man, it's the work that will carry on." Now lots of others told me the same thing. Lots of people think that he has someone he is grooming to replace him, but the ones in the know over there say no, that he is trying to perfect the system, not the man. Mr. Cortezzi,[184] the head of the American Associated Press and has been with them for 35 years in Rome, and a close personal friend of Mussolini, told me that this was just exactly what he was doing, when I told him what Mussolini had said. Everybody is so enthusiastic about his system that I don't see how it could collapse overnight.

Then I hit on what I knew was one of his two pet subjects just now; the first was about what we would call Merchant Marine. I knew Italy had been going ahead very fast with building not only Cargo Steamers, but real passenger steamers that were getting a tremendous lot of the real high-class American travel. He seemed pleased to think a Nut like me knew about that, and he went on to name the big Boats that they had built recently. He named them and the tonnage, and told of the Roma,[185] now in course of construction, which will be their largest boat.

They are now second to England in Shipbuilding, which dident make an American feel any too proud to hear. I have been told by well-informed men that he thinks that one of their only futures is on the sea, by having tremendous shipping; as he figures they can carry cheaper than anybody. Then I asked him about his No Strike plan. That is his latest and greatest hobby. He has organized the whole thing not only into an agreement but into a Trust; he has formed it into a Corporation—Labor, Capital, and the Government— and he has had a law put through where it is against the law to strike, or against the law for the Owners to cause a Lock Out. It is punishable the same as a crime is, if either side disobey. Everything has got to be submitted to this body. In a few words, they are a Supreme Court, and when they hand down their decision it is final, unless it be put up to Mussolini, as he is Minister of that too.

He said, "A strike is just like a fight out here on the Public square that is crowded with people, and two men start shooting at each other. Everything gets hit more than the men shooting at each other." Not a bad short paragraph on strikes. That is one thing about Mussolini, even in his speeches there is nothing of the long-winded about him. He gets up, hits 'em in the eye with what he wants to say, and leaves 'em groggy from shouting.

Everybody in Italy seems to think this new No Strike thing he has put in is the greatest single thing he has put over, and that it will eventually be copied by other Countries.

It certainly is working and everybody, both Capital and the labor people, is cuckoo about it. I told him I had been in England during their strike, and he said, "No Strike in Italy."

I told him the Prince of Wales and I had talked about him. He seemed pleased—that is, pleased that the Prince had spoke of him; as for me speaking of him, I don't suppose that caused him any undue gratification—the funny part about that was that he started in right away telling me about his horse and riding that morning. He went over to his desk— mind you, we have been standing up and gabbing away all this time—he touched a button and he ordered the boy to bring in something.

I thought it was mayby some old Italian vintage; I says, maybe we will get a swig of the Duce's private stock, but the Boy handed him some Photographs. He told us they had just been taken that morning, as he was riding at his Private place. They were right new and still wet. You see, I got the workings of his mind. He wanted to prove to me that where the Prince of Wales was supposed to fall off, he stayed on.

Otherwise there was no occasion of him thinking of horses or riding; but just me mentioning the Prince brought it to his mind. He sit right down to his desk and started in autographing one to me. Not only that, but put my name on it—after asking what it was—"Signor Rogers, Compliments, Mussolini," and then the date, as he was proud that the picture had been taken that very morning; so he put the place and date. It was of a Horse—and him accompanying him—making a jump; not a high jump particularly, but a good jump for Six Ministers to make at once.

I then told him that I certainly appreciated it, but that it was so far away that it dident show his face up. He set right down and picked out another one, a close-up of him and the Horse. He autographed it, but dident put my name on it, as he dident want to ask what it was again. So you see he has pride even in his Horsemanship, and he kinder wanted to show England up too I think. Well, I was mighty proud to get them and especially as I hadent asked for them. I could have come out and sold them for enough to pay for my trip to Italy— including all that you wasent supposed to pay for.

Well, he commenced to act like I was just about through, and I thanked him and told him there was only one other question that I wanted to ask him: That I knew lots of Italians over home, and that when I got back I wanted to have some message for them—what could I tell them?

Well, he laughed and put his hands on both my shoulders and said in English, "You can tell 'em Mussolini, R-e-g-u-l-a-r G-u-y. Is that right Englais?" He said, "Mussolini no Napoleon, want fight, always look mad; Mussolini, laugh, gay, like good time same as everybody else, mayby more so"—and he winked. "You tell that about Mussolini." Those are the very words he said to me to tell you. He walked over halfway across this long room and shook hands like a trained Rotarian, and I went out of there a very much agreeably surprised man.

I had felt as much at home with him as I would with Dinty Moore[186] on 46th St. I was as much surprised, Mr. President, as I was the first time I ever run onto you, when Nick took me in there, and you laughed, and pulled a few yourself, and we had a good visit, and I come out thinking you wasent as sober as you make yourself look. It's a wonderful thing to meet people and see about how they all are about the same when you can get their minds off their Lifes work.

I rushed back up to the American Embassy to tell Mr. Fletcher how nice he had been to me, for I knew he was interested in how it come out, and he had been so nice in arranging it. He was going out then to meet Mussolini at a Luncheon that Vulpy[187]—thats the fellow that went over home and settled the Italian debt. Well, Vulpy—it may not be spelled like that but it sounds like that—was giving the luncheon for Ben Strong.[188] You know Ben from New York. He is in our employ there as head of the Federal Reserve Bank, and Seamon,[189] you know, from the Treasury Department—one of Andy's Boys. But back to Mussolini.

Now you want to know just how he struck me. Well, you got to be in Italy to really understand the fellow. The trouble with America is we can't ever seem to see somebody else only through our eyes; we don't take into consideration their angle or viewpoint. Now to us he looks like he was the Tyrant and the Dictator, and that he was always posing like Napoleon, and that he was going to get his Country into war any minute. Now thats our angle on him.

Now you, Mr. President, with your one last year's suit, your speech on Economy while stepping off the Mayflower, your little quiet yet just as effective way of getting what you want done; well that and you would be just as funny to Italy as he is to us. He gets up in Public and tells Austria and Germany what to do. You have Kellogg send Mexico a note telling them what time to quit work that day. He comes into the House of Deputies over there and tells them the measures that shall be put through.

You have five or six Senators for breakfast and the same thing happens.

You see, everyone of us in the world have our audience to play to; we study them and we try and do it so it will appeal to what we think is the great majority. Now Italy likes everything put on like a Drama; they like a show, they like to have their patriotism appealed to and spoke about. They are going good and they are proud of it.

Mussolini says a lot of things publicly that sound boasting, but they are only meant for Home consumption. Why does a congressman get up and talk for an hour over home with nobody listening to him but the Stenographer? Because it's meant for the people back home.

65

It would sound crazy to the rest of America, but he knows the folks back home will eat it up. You yourself, Mr. President, know that you have to pull a lot of Apple Sauce on various occasions that your own sense of humor makes you laugh at privately. I read one over here the other day you had delivered on Decoration day about Universal Peace, and that wars were a terrible thing, and that you would lend your support to do anything to abolish them. Now that is good stuff, but take it apart, like the Italians would. They live over here among all these other people; they know there is going to be more wars; they know that it would be wonderful not to have any more, and they would lend their support, but they also know that their support is not going to do much good when they have something that some neighbor a little stronger wants.

So we all have our particular little line of Apple Sauce for each occasion. So lets be honest with ourselves, and not take ourselves too serious, and never condemn the other fellow for doing what we are doing every day, only in a different way. If this fellow Mussolini has developed this point of how to put it over to a higher Degree than any other man in modern Generations, why let's give the Kid credit.

You see, we judge all you fellows by results, you Public men. You have delivered, and if Andrews[190] don't make you sign too many papers you can stay in there as long as everybody is prosperous and doing well, because you made good. That's the way they judge this Bird over here. If he died tomorrow Italy would always be indebted to him for practically four years of peace and prosperity. Not a bad record to die on at that; but this Guy keeps on getting better all the time. He is the only idealist that ever could make it work.

Some over home say a Dictator is no good! yet every successful line of business is run by a Dictator.

This Fellow has been to Italy just what Henry Ford has been to all those old Ash cans and empty bottles and old pig iron; he molded them into a working machine by his own mind and Dictatorship. Your Political Parties; how many men run them? Say, Penrose[191] told everybody in your Party how to set their watch every day. You think the Democrats as a party will pick out the next Presidential Candidate; say, it will be one man that will name the Candidate. So everything is really done by Dictatorship, if you just sum it down. Dictator form of Government is the greatest form of Government there is, if you have the right Dictator. Well these folks have certainly got him.

Now as to what will happen when he is no more, why of course no one can tell. But as I said before, he is trying to so perfect the thing that it will go along without him, the same as our founders made our Constitution almost Fool Proof. Of course there will be guys pop up and try to improve on Mussolini's ideas after he has gone, the same as we have 'em every day trying to monkey with ours, or add more things to it or something. But if it's good and the people living under it see the benefits of it every day, the same as we see the benefits of ours every day, why I think the general principals of his government will carry on without him. Then you don't want to forget that that Castor oil will live on after he has gone, and that, applied at various times with proper disscretion, is bound to do some good from every angle. You never saw a man where as many people and as many classes of people were for him as they are this fellow. Of course he has opposition, but it is of such a small percentage that it wouldent have a chance to get anywhere even if they would let it pop its head up.

Now just a little bit about the man. He is just 42 years old now, his Father was a Blacksmith and as a Kid he was his assistant. His father was always a Socialist and Mussolini grew up a Socialist. Lots of people think that he is not an educated man, but he is: why I never read of a man that had studied and thought and read as much as he has. His Mother was a school teacher herself and he first went to school to her. He afterwards taught French at several places in Switzerland; he speaks also German and Russian.

He has been an editor of various Socialist papers for years. He was thrown out of the Socialist Party because he was for Italy going into the war on the side of the Allies; he fought through war till wounded by shrapnel in about 40 places. He has been in every Jail in Switzerland when he was a Socialist, also in Austria and put out of there when released. The only way he could get in again was to have Italy declare war and go in with the Army. In Italy he has been in most of their less exclusive Jails. In fact that is how those Socialists lived, just from one jail to another—oh, yes, and he can play the Violin too. So he is a kind of a modern Nero; in case Rome has a fire he is all set to do some violining. I don't know how good he can play—in fact, we don't know how good Nero played—but I guess he can play good enough for a fire. I hope he don't play Valencia during the fire to add to their woe.

He is quite a Fencer; that is that game they have with Swords, and they also are supposed to fight Duels, which are started by one man slapping the other in the face with his glove, which is folded up in his hand. That is the worst you ever get hurt in those duels, unless you happen to fall on your own sword. Well he does that every day, getting ready to try and puncture somebody's middle.

He has a wife and three children—the oldest is a daughter of 15, a son and another daughter. He likes to get in a big high-powered car

67

and drive it himself, and go fast. So in addition to being Minister of Interior, Exterior, Minister of Earth, Minister of Sky, Minister of Labor, Minister of Capital, now on account of this Automobiling he is also Minister of Traffic Cops. When the Cabinet holds a meeting he sits in 6 Chairs and crowds the other fellow pretty near out of the room. He is a tough Guy when he wants to be. He will fight you or kiss you, just whichever you choose.

He has put everybody in Italy to work and he worked harder than any of them doing it; and anybody that has ever been to Italy before knows that anyone that can put them to work, even if he never did anything else, should follow Caesar into the hall of fame. That is one thing that will kinder react against him with these Italians over home there that generally come back to Italy to loaf. I am going to tell you Birds right now, you ain't going to loaf on this Guy. Everybody is doing something. France works too. When they see an American they work on him. I never saw a single beggar on the street. I was in the Gallery of the Chamber of Deputies when he come in to make a report on their Foreign Policy and various other odds and ends. He spoke of the Locarno Pact[192] and said, "The architecture of the Locarno Pact is very simple. It is just the case of two Nations, France and Germany, agreeing not to attack each other. But because these two don't believe each other after they sign, there are two others to guarantee the pledge; and that is England and Italy. Regarding the value of the pact, it must rest on the spirit of the pact, and I think we all know that the spirit of Locarno has suffered certain drawbacks lately. The treaty between Russia and Germany[193] since has clouded the issue. The spirit of Peace is a wonderful thing, but let's not put our head under the sand." Now these are the exact words, as I had the translator of the Embassy make me a exact copy in English.

"Emigration—I am not an enthusiast on the subject of emigration. It is a sad and painful thing to endure when you emigrate millions of your most courageous—the strongest, the most audacious. We have an institute now to finance Italian labor abroad, and it has given good account of itself by colonization in the Argentine and, to be more precise, in the southern Zone of the Rio Grande.

"We have been accused of being imperialistic. I am comforted by the study of books, which are the common inheritance of culture, that every human being has some imperialistic tendencies. Every living being who wants to live must develop a certain will or power; otherwise they will vegetate and will be the prey of stronger people. One hears certain beautiful phrases: 'International solidarity'; 'brotherhood of race'; 'cordiality of relations.' But the reality is different. Disarmament is great, but it must be total; otherwise it is only an ugly comedy. I say total, meaning on Land, on Sea and in the Air. Then Italy will disarm."

Those are the principal high spots of the speech, and he had 'em tearing up the seats when he finished. He is doing an awful lot of treaty signing on his own. The week I was there he signed 18 different Treaties with Yugoslavia[194] alone. That's a treaty to every inhabitant. Greece has them a little small time Mussolini over there, and he had just sent over wanting some ships and stuff in the way of war material,[195] but of course was a little short of jack. So Mussolini told them to "go up to Italy's shipyards and get what they wanted, PROVIDED they would use disscretion in picking out a side to fight on in the next war."

He says he won't need any treaties with Austria. "We can take care of them any time we want to." He has got France afraid to go to the door and put the cat out at night. But as a man here said that ought to know—I can't divulge his name, here, Mr. President, as this letter may fall into the hands of the Democrats, but I will tell you when I get home who it was, you know him—he told me, "This is a very smart fellow. He don't want to take his country into war; he wants to build it up. If he can keep these others guessing, so much the better; but he is not going to pull any Napoleon stuff; he is too smart for that."

I think, personally, that he has made a close study of History and found where each one of these other Napoleon's foot slipped, and he makes a red mark around it; and every few days he goes to these various Histories and looks to see if he is near one of those red marks, and if he is, why he "Goes away out around 'em, Shep," like a Sheep-herder's dog. He says to himself, I am not going to pull the same bone that fellow did.

Even the Church is strong for him; he has done more to bring on good feeling between them and the Country than ever before. The Pope[196] likes him; the King[197] likes him.

He is very generous with the King, and there relations are very cordial; and don't get the idea that this King hasent got his following. I learned something over there—this little King is tremendously popular too; they like him. He made a big hit with his record in the war, the King did; he stayed right up at the front with the men all the time. If I get home and find out what Bull Montana[198] thinks of Mussolini, why, I will have the entire Italian opinion.

Now a few words of how the Country was when he first took it over. There just wasent any government at all; The Socialists had taken over the Factories, the owners had nothing to do with them;

it was dangerous to walk on the streets. A returned Soldier was their particular mark; they jeered at him. One Minister would be at the head of the Government a few weeks and then they would throw him out. To say it was a Revolution all over the country would be putting it mildly. Well, to sum it up in a few words, from all I can gather about it, it was just another Chicago, and him and castor oil cleared it all in less than four years. I don't believe we ever had anything just like him; Roosevelt—no doubt Mussolini has studied him—but Roosevelt was a Stand Patter to the side of this Guy. Course I don't think he is as great as Roosevelt, because I don't think anybody was as great as Roosevelt, but this Gent is a kind of a cross between Roosevelt, Red Grange, Babe Ruth,[199] when the Babe is really good; the elder Lafolette, a touch of Borah, Bryan of '96, Samuel Gomperts and Tunny.[200] Now you can scramble all those concoctions up into one and you will just have a kind of a rough idea about this Roman. I hope that makes it clear to you. Oh, yes, as we come in he gave us the Facisti salute—you look out straight and point your arm kinder up and out. They say it's a salute that originally come from the old Romans, but personally I think they copped it from Old Doc Munyon's There-is-hope salute.[201] Traffic policemen over home have been giving it for years, but nobody ever paid any attention to them.

He is funny, too, this Guy. I read one of his speeches where he was talking about a certain law that should be changed; he said, "Why this law is no good; it's just like the skin on a fat man's belly; you can pull it about wherever you want it. It should be changed." Somebody sent him a painting of himself that they had done in oil, and he said, "They should render the salad oil out of it; that's worth more than the Picture." It was new and just oozing oil.

Well, I must be closing; I may see a few more people over here and write you about them, but this was the main one I come to get, and anybody I see from now on will just be like slumming. I want to write you sometime about the wine carts coming down from the mountains, and oh, a lot of things about Rome. Oh, it's got a lot of history. They got buildings that look pretty near as old as some of those in Boston.

It's just full of History and wine, Rome is. Now this castor-oil recipe—if you don't do anything about that why let me know, because the Mexican Government will grab that in a minute. I want to write you later, too, about some of the other help around the Embassy. Everybody is mighty fine and right on the job. Well, that's about all I can think of for the present that castor oil has done for Italy.

Your devoted temporary Roman,

W. R.

My Dear Mr. President: Calvin, I wish you could see Rome. It's the oldest uncivilized Town in the world. New York is just as uncivilized, but it's not as old as Rome. Rome has been held by every Nation in the World at one time or another for no reason at all. Between you and I, I think some of them give it up without much of a struggle.

Rome has more Churches and less preaching in them than any City in the World. Everybody wants to see where Saint Peter was buried. But nobody wants to try to live like him.

There is 493 Guidebooks sold to every Testament. They would rather take Baedeker's[202] word than Moses'.

The headliners in Roman History is Julius Caesar, Mark Antony and Nero. Then Mussolini come along and made Bush Leaguers out of all of them.

Rome was built on seven hills. Every prominent Roman had a little hill all his own. History records, and local gossip has added to history, that coming home after a hard and exciting night at the baths, there has been Romans that dident find the right hill. That's what made Roman history interesting. There is only six of these hills left today. Some Roman went out of the back window so fast one night that he took the hill with him. That's the inside story. But of course present History says that the Barbarians took not only all the assembled Romans but the hill as well with them.

I tried to find out who the Barbarians were. From the best that I could learn, Barbarians were a race of people that stole from you. If you stole from the barbarians, you were indexed in your History as a Christian.

Now of these six hills left, the Pope has one, Volpi—the man that settled the Italian Debt—has one, Garabaldi[203] grabbed off one for his personal statue. A filling station and Spagetti joint has one, Mussolini copped the highest one for the duce himself, and the last and lowest one the King has. You wouldent hardly call it a hill; it's more of a mound.

Rome wasent built in a day. It's not a Miami Beach by any means. All Tourist agencies advise you to spend at least 10 days seeing it. The Hotels advise you to take four months.

You see, Cal, that is why I am trying to find out all I can for you. I think people in our position have to look to our historical as well as Political Knowledge. So while as everyone admits you are excellently equipped politically—I don't know of a man better fortified—a little historical knowledge would do you no harm. You see, up around Boston you have seen Plymouth Rock and Boston Common and the old graveyard going up the hill toward the Capitol, But those things mean nothing to a real historian. You have seen the spot where Paul Revere come riding down hollering, "The Dam has broke!" But they had guys in Rome that invented Dams. You see, to a Roman events like those would be classed as topical today.

Well, after I finished with Mussolini, I decided to take up Rome. Of course Mussolini naturally come first, for he "made Rome what it is today; I hope he's satisfied." You see, chances are up there in Vermont you studied a little history. But you can't get much out of history in Vermont. You can't get much out of Vermont anyway. There is an awful lot of difference between reading something, and actually seeing it, for you can never tell till you see it, just how big a liar History is.

In other words, Rome is really not what it's cracked up to be. History was no more right in reporting the happenings of Rome than it has been in some of the Cities we have heard of. Now everybody goes to Rome on account of its old historical record. Now you know and I know it ain't History that you are out to study. You are out to make History. What you want to plan is, some day some Guy will be studying you instead of you studying him. Any Yap can read what somebody else has done; but can he get out and do something himself, that anybody would read about, even if they dident have anything else to read?

Now what I wanted to do was to cover Rome from a human-interest point of view. In other words, I wanted to see something that was alive. I am, I bet you, the only one that ever visited the city that dident run myself ragged dragging from one old Church to another, and from one old Oil Painting to the next. In the first place, I don't care anything about Oil Paintings. Ever since I struck a dry hole near the old home ranch in Rogers County, Oklahoma I have hated oil, in the raw, and all it subsiduaries. You can even color it up, and it don't mean anything to me. I don't want to see a lot of old Pictures. If I wanted to see old Pictures I would get D. W. Griffith[204] to revive the Birth of a Nation.[205] That's the best old Picture there is. I wouldent mind seeing the Four Horsemen[206] again. But this thinking that everything was good just because it was old is the Apple sauce. They only produced a few great men, so why should every picture they painted be great?

Say, Charles Dana Gibson and Herbert Johnson[207] can assemble 'em good enough for me. They may never hang in the Louvre, But they sho do dangle from the front page of many an old News stand. So I am not going to kid myself and I am not going to kid you either, Cal. I know your and my tastes are about alike, and when I was looking at things I was a-thinking all the time of you, and wondering if you wouldent size the thing up just about along my lines.

Of course, every once in a while something comes up in Washington they think is more or less of an Artistic nature and naturally, as head of the Government, you have to go there or appear before them and mayby say a few words pertaining partly to the subject at hand. Well, you get one of the secretaries there to dig you up the night before a few names and dates and so-called achievements along the line that this convention or Society is working on, and you get away with it.

But that's one beautiful thing about our association, you and I— we don't kid each other. We know about 9-10ths of the stuff going on under the guise of Art is the Banana Oil. They call it Art to get to take off the clothes. When you ain't nothing else, you are an Artist. It's the one thing you can claim to be and nobody can prove you ain't. No matter how you build anything and how you painted anything, if it accidentally through lack of wars or rain happened to live a few hundreds of years, why its Art now. Maby when the Guy painted it at the time he never got another contract. Maby some of the Pictures they have now was at that time thrown away in an old cellar because they wasent thought good enough to show, and they laid there all these years and somebody dug 'em out and now they are the Old Masters. I know how it is with you, you have had a hundred Movies brought to the White House to be shown to you, and I bet you never been in the Smithsonian Institution since you first went there as Vice President, when you dident have anything else to do. So when I tell you about Rome I just want you to picture it as it is, not as it is in the guidebooks, but as an ordinary hard-boiled American like you and I would see it.

Now we call Rome the seat of Culture, but somebody stole the chair. Today it has no more culture than Minneapolis or Long Beach, California. They live there in Rome amongst what used to be called Culture, but that don't mean a thing. Men in Washington you know yourself, Calvin, live where Washington and Jefferson and Hamilton lived, but as far as the good it does them, they just as well have the Capitol down at Claremore, Oklahoma—and, by the way, I doubt if Claremore would take it; there is a Town that has never had a set-back. So, you see, Association has nothing to do with culture.

I know Englishmen that have had the same well-bred Butler all their lives and they are just as rude as they ever were. Why, do you know, one of the most cultured men I ever saw come from Texas, and where he learned it the Lord only knows. It's just one of those freaks of Nature like a Rose among Prickly Pears.

73

Then another thing you got to take into consideration. If a town had any culture and Tourists commenced hitting it, Your culture is gone. Tourists will rub it out of any town. Now you take the Tourists. There is one of the hardest working business that you could possibly adopt—the business of trying to see something. They will leave a nice comfortable home with all conveniences, and they will get them a ticket to Europe and from then on they stop being a human; they just turn sheep. The Guide is the sheep herder, and about the same fellow the regular sheep herder is on a ranch. You ask him anything outside his regular routine and you are going to spoil his pleasure for the day, besides not finding out the answer yourself.

After a bunch of Tourists have been out a couple of weeks and get broke in good, the guide don't have to do much; they know about when to bunch up and start listening. They kinder pull in together like a covey of quail and form a sort of a half circle while the Guide tells them what he has read in their guide books. They listen and mark it off and move on over to another picture. They come dragging into the hotel at night, and you would think they had walked here from America. If you asked them to do that hard a day's work in their own towns they would think you was cuckoo.

Then they dress for dinner. They couldent possibly go down in the dining room without the little Organdie on. Even the men put on Monkey Suits that at home you couldent get him into one with an elephant hook. Why anybody can't act the same away from home and enjoy just as much freedom as they do there is more than I will ever know.

But I want to tell you they are taking this sight-seeing serious. It's no pleasure; it's a business. You speak to one of them after he has been a-touring all day, and start to tell him something, he will start looking up on the wall for some old Frescoe's or a stained-glass window. You can tell a Tourist after a long tour; they have held a Guidebook in one hand so long they have learned to do everything else with the other hand. Everyone of them when they get home from Rome can tell you where Caesar and Nero were born, and not a one of them can tell you, Calvin, where you or Borah or Dawes first saw the political light. They have seen the Boragzzi Galleries and the Louvre, but think the Smithsonian Institution is a Clinic and the Field Museum[208] is a branch of the great Department Store.

They saw the place where Nero tuned up his old bass viol just before the third alarm was turned in—they say that, but they never heard Albert Spalding[209] play either with or without the accompaniment of a fire. Then they get up early in the morning to start out to see more old Churches. Now a Church is all right, and they are the greatest things we have in our lives, but not for a steady diet. They figure the earlier they can get you out, the more Churches you can see that day. If you are not interested in old Churches, you can stop off and see Rome between trains.

Then they go in great for old ruins. Now I know you have lived up around those old farmhouses in New England long enough to feel about ruins just about like I do. A ruin don't just exactly spellbind me; I don't care how long it has been in the process of ruination. I kept trying to get 'em to show me something that hadent started to rue yet.

They got a lot of things they call Forums. They are where the Senators used to meet and debate—on disarmament, I suppose. They say there was some bloody mob scenes and fights in there. Well, that's one thing they got us licked on. Calling each other a liar and heaving an inkstand is about the extent of our Senatorial gladiators' warlike accomplishments.

I dident know before I got there, and they told me all this—that Rome had Senators. Now I know why it declined. There is quite an argument there over the exact spot of Caesar's Death. Some say that Caesar was not slain in the Senate; they seem to think that he had gone over to a Senatorial Investigation meeting at some Committee room, and that that is where Brutus gigged him. The moral of the whole thing seems to be to stay away from investigations.

I also picked up a little scandal there that I know you won't turn a deaf ear to. About this particular case, they are saying around Rome now, but they hope it don't get back to any of his people, that Brutus was Caesar's natural son, and that Cassius was a sort of a brother-in-law without Portfolio. Then they showed where Mark Anthony delivered his oration, which, as it wasent written till 500 years after he was supposed to say it, there was some chance there of misinterpretation. I have heard some of our Public men's speeches garbled in next morning's paper.

Then they speak of a Cicero. I don't know exactly what he did. His name sounds kinder like he was a window dresser. Then there was the intellectual tracks of Vergil. I guess you had a crack at him while you was up at Amherst.[210] Vergil must have been quite a fellow, but he dident know enough to put his stuff in English like Shakespeare did, so you don't hear much of him anymore, only in high school and roasting-ear Colleges, where he is studied more and remembered less than any single person. I bet you yourself right now, Mr. President, don't know over three of Vergil's words. E Pluribus Unum will just about let you out. I never even got to him in school, and I remember that much. Ask Vare when he gets in there to quote you some of Vergil.

There is quite a few of those old Forums besides the Senate one. Evidently they were afflicted with a House of Representatives, a Supreme Court and a Foreign Relations Committee. 'Course it's just a lot of old broken-down Marble now. Most of the old pieces are big enough so the Tourists can't carry them away; that's the only reason they are there. A lot of them are being torn down to put in modern plumbing.

That's one thing the Tourists have done anyway—they have improved Europe's plumbing. Rome had more Art and less bath-tubs than any city outside of Moscow. Romans were great to bathe collectively, but individually they were pretty dirty. Funny thing about Roman baths. You see Pictures of them, but you never saw a Picture with anyone in the water. They were great people to drape themselves around on marble slabs. But I don't think they even had any water in the pools. Bathing was a kind of an excuse to get neglije with each other.

You remember the picture they always have where one old Roman, or some of those foreigners, got sore and come out and was standing between two big pillars and was pushing them apart. Well, that was an old Senator got sore during a Filibuster, and he just went out and he puffed and he puffed and he blowed the house in. Boy, they had Senators in them days. Little John Sargent[211] would have been a Page boy among that gang. They used to throw these pillars at each other during debate.

Rome has what they call a river. It's the Tiber, and of all the overrated things! You would think a River that is good enough to get into History for all these years would have something to back it up, wouldn't you? Old-time History don't say a word about the Arkansaw or the South Canadian or Grand River or the Verdigris,[212] and here this Tiber couldent be a tributary to one of those. Besides, the Tiber don't flow; it just oozes along. Nobody was ever drowned in it; but lots of old Settlers have bogged down in it and lost their lives. You can walk across it anywhere if you don't mind getting muddy. You can't fish in it. The mud is so thick in the water that the Fish can't see the bait, and when they do see it it's so muddy they won't eat it.

They used to have a wall around the City but the people got to climbing over it so much they just sorter neglected it and let it run down. It got so the wall wouldent keep the people from getting out. They would climb over and go off to some other place. You can't keep people in a place with a wall. If they don't like a town they will leave it. Look at Sing Sing.[213] They got a better wall than Rome even thought they had, and still very few stay in there. That wall system

76

is a failure and always was. Walls are all right to put your back to if somebody is fighting you; it keeps you from backing any further away from them, and sometimes makes you fight when if it wasent for the wall you would keep backing. One thing I will say for Rome—they have kept up the gates of the old wall. They have let all the rest of the wall fall down, but the Gates are kept in very good repair. 'Course you can walk around them and get in without coming through the gate, but I guess they never thought of anybody doing that.

The whole of Rome seems to have been built, painted and decorated by one man; that was Michelangelo. If you took everything out of Rome that was supposed to have been done by Michelangelo,[214] Rome would be as bare of Art as Los Angeles.

He was a picture Painter, Sculptor, a House painter, both inside and out—for in those days they painted the ceilings. He was an Architect, a Landscape Gardener, Interior Decorator, and I wouldent doubt if he dident strum a mean Guitar. It's hard to tell you what all that fellow was. We have over home today no single person that compares with him, not even in California. He was a Stanford White[215] in drawing up all the local Blue Prints of his day. He was the Charley Russel[216] of the old paintbrush; but he had Charley beat, for Charley never has had to resort to painting the inside of roofs of buildings. Charley will set down and paint, but he won't lay down on his back and paint.

Then Michel used to do what they called Mosaics. That's a kind of a colored Cross-Word Puzzle. He had never done any of this and they asked him one time if he would do some of it. It seems the local Mosaicker was on a strike for more wages and easier designs, so they give Angelo a handful of these little blocks—this was in his off time while he wasent working on St. Peters and St. Pauls and the 48 other Churches he was painting and Sculpturing, besides a few odds and ends about town where he would pick up off jobs.

Well, he took these little cubes and squares up there and he worked every one of them; every word he got right without a Dictionary or a Scenario, and he got the prize the next day in the paper for working out the best Mosaic puzzle of his time, and he wasent even playing. You know, an awful lot of his finest work like the Dome in St. Peters, he had to lay on his back away up there on a scaffold, and on account of having so much work ahead of him, he would lay up there and he put those things in during his sleep. Well, he certainly got even with everybody for it all. For you have to lay down on your back to look up at it.

Now there is one thing that they are going to have a little trouble cramming down me. How could they lay on their back and make

77

that mosiac stick up there? It would be like trying to play checkers upside down. What's going to hold 'em up there?

'Course you kinder got to let that go under the heading of Miracles, for Miracles was supposed to happen around that time. There hasent been many lately unless the Democrats are fortunate enough to scare up one.

This Michelangelo was just about the whole thing in Rome in those days. He was sorter the Senator Borah of Rome. You see, an Artist in those days was the whole thing. People's minds run to Art and Wild Animals. A man of commerce or trade or business—he dident mean much; he dident have any more chance than Farmers relief; he was just a minority Stockholder. They would just tolerate him up to the time they needed some Lion bait, and then his name was liable to drop out of the Directory. Henry Ford or Judge Gary or Charley Schwab, or either Young or Old John D.[217]—any of those men of Commerce they wouldent have meant a thing in Roman days. If Ford couldent have proved that one of those things come under the heading of Art, he would have had no more social Status than a motorman. They would have just used any and all of the above named gentry as grooms for the lions to keep 'em slicked up till Sunday. They would have had as much chance getting into the 400 of Rome as a Democrat has eating breakfast with you, Mr. President. It would be worse than a Yankee trying to break into Charleston, South Carolina, Society.

Art and religion ruled the day, and as none of our present-day financiers are familiar or in any way connected with either Art or religion or any of their allied industries, why, it looks like our Multimillionaires would have been just sitting in the bleachers socially.

But everything travels in cycles. Art took a tumble and was replaced by Low profit and quick turnover. Art not only was relegated to the rear but it just naturally passed out with no mourners. It dident appear again until what is known as the Bud Fisher and Rube Goldberg[218] period. Ziegfeld took Michelangelo's statues, took some of the fat off of them with a diet of lamb chops and pineapple, and he and a Confederate named Ben Ali Hagen[219] brought the statues to life, only with better figures, and the only marble about them was from the ears north.

But even to this day, if a Picture or a piece of Statuary is losing interest and they can't get anybody to look at it any more, why, the remark is secretly whispered around that is was really done by Angelo on one of his days off. Then the Tourists commence reaching for their Guidebooks.

Not to have the Angelo brand on your Sculptured hitching rack was to be a Plebian among the Romans.

Henry Ford has always received the credit for what we call mass production. But I want to tell you that if Michelangelo even turned out all the Statues that they say he did—that's even if he dident paint at all—why, he was the originator of Mass Production, and not Uncle Henry.

There was another fellow about that time too. You know things kinder run in bunches, or rather imitations. So naturaly Angelo would have imitators. When the shareholders in a Church couldent get Angelo to paint or sculp for 'em, why, they went out and got a fellow named Rafael.[220] He was the first one that ever billed himself "Just as good."

Well, between him and Angelo they just about painted Rome red. They confined their Paintings mostly to Bible Characters, which was a very smart thing to do, as nobody knew just how these Characters should look; and in painting one you could always make him look any way you wanted him too, and if someone criticized it, you would always have the Alibi, "Well, that's my interpretation of the character."

I want to tell you right know it's the modern painter that has the tough job. He has to make 'em look enough like the Millionaire's wife that the visitors can recognize her, and still make her look like she thinks she looks. When you can do that, then thats art. Why, those old Characters they painted they could paint with or without Whiskers, One-eyed, bald-headed or long-haired, any way they wanted: they dident have to make 'em look like anything. Just turn out a Picture—that was all they had to do.

These two Boys that I speak of were doing practically everything in Rome in those days; if you dident give them a retaining fee, you wasent having any Art done. Oh, of course maby there was a little Bootleg Art going on around in some of the side streets somewhere, but nothing highpowered. In fact Art was a closed Corporation. If some outsider come in with what he thought was a painting, why, about the best he could do with it would be to get it on some Magazine cover or a front piece for the next Program for the Chariot race.

Along about the period of these Painters and Mud Dobbers come another sort of an Artistic breed called the Gladiators. A fellow was a Gladiator as long as he remained alive—that's what made him glad. Saturday night was always a rather ticklish time in the life of a Gladiator, for that is when they generally announced the entries for the Bulldogging contest with the Lions the following day. If you defeated your Lion you were allowed to be Glad for another week.

These Romans loved blood. What money is to an American,

blood was to a Roman. A Roman was never so happy as when he saw somebody bleeding. That was his sense of humor, just like ours is. If we see a fellow slip and fall and maby break his leg, why, that's a yell to us; or his hat blow off and he can't get it. Well, that's the way the Romans were. Where we like to see you lose your hat, they loved to see you leave a right arm and a left leg in the possession of a Tiger and then try to make the fence unaided.

The Emperor set in his box, and a lot of Ladies set in another great big Box, and during the festivities they would announce with their thumbs whether the man was to go on to his death or let him live. The women had the first guess, but the Emperor he had the veto power; he passed on the things as final. You see, they used their thumbs for something besides buttoning up their clothes. If they held their thumbs down, you passed out Poco Pronto; but if they held them up, why, you left your phone and address where you could be reached the following Sunday afternoon. There was no Dempsey stuff of four years between combats, no dickering over terms. The gate receipts went to the Emperor and you went to the cemetery.

'Course this old Colosseum is a great old building. They have stole enough off of it to build everything else in Rome. Poor Mussolini come in so late in history that there wasent anything left for him at all. Everything in Rome was stolen from somebody at some time. It's just a question of who's got it last.

That's why I say there is nothing new there; we got everything over home, only bigger and better. Take Vesuvius, for instance: I know that it buried a City, but that means nothing to me or to you. I have in the past year seen lots of buried Cities over home. Over-advertising has buried more Cities than Vesuvius could bury if she run over every day. Political Parties have buried more platforms the day after election, both the winners and losers, than Vesuvius will ever hear of. Vesuvius destroys by spontaneous combustion—that is, heat and friction within itself. Now you mean to tell me it can improve on the Democrats for spontaneous combustion? A buried city is the last thing I want to see. I want something that's a-living.

Now there is a forum there called Stargens, or something like that, and it's down in the ground with a high wall around it, and a lot of old Marble columns broken off and standing and laying around. Well, they have a habit of taking all the old stray cats and the neighbors feed them. It has now become known as the Forum of the Cats. Now to me that was a real place. Here was something alive. I used to walk down there to see what the old kitties were doing, and at night I went two or three times. You could see an old tomcat setting up on top of a Roman column where maby Mark Anthony had delivered one of his monologues. This old Tabby would be squatting up there, howling for no reason at all, just like a typical politician, and just as much sense to it too. Now that was great to me to see those Cats. I don't want to convey any disrspect to those who have passed beyond, but I would rather see one live Cat than a dozen dead Romans.

No, sir, Calvin, you are standing guard over not only the best little patch of ground in all the various Hemispheres but we got it on 'em even when it comes to things to see, if we could just make these Locoed Tourists believe it. Why, say, if the Mississippi ever flowed through, for instance, Switzerland, why, there wouldent be enough dry ground left to yodle in. Their little rivers, if they ever saw it, would flow right into a rain barrel and stay there.

Why, if they had Niagara Falls they would have had 85 wars over it at various times to see who would be allowed to charge admission to see it. If they get to monkeying with us we will lose 'em in the Mammoth Cave.[221] They rave over Venice; there's nothing there but water. Why, Louisiana has more water in their cellars than the whole Adriatic Sea. And the Grand Canyon—well, I just don't want to hurt their feelings talking about it. No, sir, Europe has nothing to recommend it but its old age, and the Petrified forest in Arizona makes a Sucker out of it for old age. Why, that forest was there and doing business before Nero took his first Violin lesson.

You take the Guides and the Grapes out of Europe and she is just a Sahara. It's great for you to see, if somebody is paying for it, or paying you to do it. But just as a pure educational proposition or pastime, it ain't there,

yours devotedly,

WILL.

Venice, June 7, '26.

Dear Mr. Coolidge:

I must tell you about Venice. Say what a fine swamp that Venice Italy turned out to be. I stepped out of the wrong side of a Venice Taxicab and they were three minutes fishing me out. They have taximeters on the Gondolar's, so many knots are so many liras. The greatest drivers in the world are these Skippers on these Venice "Hansoms." They can take two of these crafts and make 'em pass in a bath tub, and never touch either. There is no such thing as a bent fender on one of those hulls. The Captain, the Pilot, the Cabin Boy and the crew are one and the same on the Venice rapid transit. The Chouffers can row so quiet that you cant hear a sound, till you start to pay him and dont tip enough, and then you would think it was a drunk seal in an Aquarium.

I got seasick crossing an alley. I saw a fellow there from New York trying to engage third class passage from the Depot to the Hotel. Condilier drivers hate the Motor boats and when no one is looking they just casually and accidentally slip an oar into the propeller as they pass. If you love to have someone row you in a boat you will love Venice. But dont try to walk or they will be searching for you with grappling hooks.

Yours for dry land,

WILL.

NICE, France, around June 8, '26.
(It's pronounced neece, not nice; they have no word
for nice in French.)

My Dear Mr. President: It's been quite a while since I heard from you; but I guess it's just as well, because I wouldent have known any more after you had written. You haven't been what I would call extravagant with your news, and what little I got I had to pick up out of the Paris Edition of the New York Herald or the Paris Edition of the Chicago Tribune. Both have the same news from the same Republican angle. I wish I could get Mr. Ochs[222] to start a Times over here so we would get the Democratic slant on some of the news.

These papers won't publish a Democrat's name in the recent arrivals at Hotels. 'Course there may be an excuse for that, the Democrats may not be going to Hotels. I guess they are living in what they call Pensions, as they dident get in on any Pensions after the war— the war between the Democrats and Republicans in '65—and as they have always had to help pay 'em, they wanted to see what one was like. 'Course the news that we have been getting lately from over there is not of a nature that would make you any to enthusiastic about relating it. [223]

The papers over here had an awful lot about you and that signing of that paper of Andrew's.[224] 'Course the Republican Alibi over here for you was that you dident know what you was signing. Now I dident like that. I am not blaming you, it was not your fault. But where is John Sargent, the tall sycamore from Vermont? What does he think we dug him out of the granite and brought him in alleged civilization for if it wasent for just this very thing—just to watch what you clapped your John Henry on? He is supposed to watch every paper and see before you sign it that there is no political catch in it whereby there may be any votes lost in November, '28. So if

John can't look after our interests any better than that, why, we will have him get the old return ticket out and dust it off and let him go back and hibernate with the maples. Even Dudley Field Malone or Darrow[225] could advise us that bad.

I read about Borah up there in Baltimore in his speech.[226] They made a big to-do over that over here. It wasent on account of the political significance of the thing. It was because Borah made it. There is an awful lot of people here that thinks that Borah is our Prime Minister.

Now the Minister over here in all these Countries is the main one; the King or the President or any of those have to sit in the Spectators' Gallery. But the Minister is the grapes. So they think Borah is the Minister, or power behind the throne; that whatever he says goes. 'Course the whole idea is a laugh and ridiculous to me, but the funny part about it is there is a lot of people right over home think the same thing. 'Course I try to set 'em right all I can, but when I tell 'em that he is only a Senator they won't believe it, for they have heard about Senators. In fact a lot of these Countries are troubled with them, too, and they won't believe a man could be so prominent and well known and still be nothing but a Senator.

But they can't understand our Democratic way in America, where we give every man a chance no matter how low his station in life may be. They can't understand a race of people as big as we are paying any attention to just a Senator. So it looks like we will have to give Borah the title of Prime Minister just to stop us Americans explaining that there is no such office, officially. Now if Borah looked the thing over and jumped with the Drys, just between you and I, if I was you I would hunt the same springboard and make exactly the same leap. He looks far ahead, that old boy does, and when he chooses sides you better grab your glove and ball and go over and play with him.

Now he has sit there all year and listened to the loud static of the wets, and he heard a terrible lot of weird and loud noises; but he just kinder diagnosed the case and said there is hundreds of yells coming out of the same mouth. In other words, for every 500 noises there was really only one vote. Well, as you know, he is a man kinder like yourself in that respect. You-all have generally been able to detect a voting prospect through a brick wall with no windows. So if he has made his choice, I believe if I was you I would climb right out of the old shell not only with the old hackneyed gag, "I am for law enforcement." That don't mean anything.

Naturally, any man that holds office is for law enforcement. You fellows can't keep on getting by on that old Alibi. There is too many of you now trying to stand on the line between the wets and the drys, and it's too narrow for all of you. Some of you have got to jump one way or the other. In other words, you got to make it plain.[227] Every one of you have got to take to the open and run for your lives.

You see, that is how Borah keeps ahead of all you other Politicians. He is never living European and American plan both at the same time. When he arrives at a hotel he announces his Plan. Now I would do it in such a way that it don't look like you are copying him. I wouldent, for instance, go to Baltimore and make the same speech; but I would pick some nice soft spot at some big affair when there is no big Murder case or Ball game or Divorce case going on in the papers, plant it when things are dull, and if you do it right, even the pictorials may use it for a couple of paragraphs, and then you will be all set.

I should think you fellows would want to be right out flat-footed on anything. It would relieve my conscience to know that I dident have to walk the eaves of the Flatiron Building[228] on everything that come up. So I would just use Bill as a barometer, and when you see he is ready to climb on anything, you go get a front seat right quick before anybody knows you were watching him.

Well I will stop, but just think this over.

Yours devotedly,

W. R.

CABLEGRAM. RUSH
MONTE CARLO, Monaco, June 22, '26

PRESIDENT OF U. S.,
WHITE HOUSE.

Please send money. Unexpected Diplomatic relations have suddenly arisen here which no one could foresee. Please rush, as French Taxi Driver is waiting. They are unusualy impatient when you owe them.

WILLROG.

GENEVA, Switzerland, June 23.

MR. PRESIDENT,
WHITE HOUSE,
WASHINGTON, D. C, ...

Have found Pullman car window that will open without crew of Porters. Biggest discovery made in Europe so far on entire trip. Take it up with Hoover.[229] In case Lowden[230] comes out against you we can use this against his Company by marriage.

Yours affectionately,

WILL.

MR. PRESIDENT,

WHITE HOUSE,

Dear President: I arrived in Paris late at night. The next day we had Briand Premier for breakfast; Herriot[231] Premier for Lunch; Poincaré[232] for Dinner; and woke up the next morning and Briand is back in again. This is not a Government; it's an old-fashioned Movie, where they flash on the screen: "Two minutes, please, while we change Premiers." I have had a date to interview every one of them, but they were thrown out before the Interview time come due. I acted on your suggestion and proposed Abd-el-Krim,[233] but he turned it down flat; said he would go back to war before he would take a job like that. You may have to send Butler or Pinchot.

Yours same as ever,

W. R.

Special Cable[234]

CALCOOL, *Whitewashhouse:*

PARIS, June 24.—They limit you here in Paris to a two-course dinner. Meats, vegetables, soups, fish and dessert are not counted in either course.

It's two courses outside of any of these, so it's not such a hardship on the ravenous Americans as was at first expected.[235]

WILLROG.

CANNES, France, June 25, '26.

THE PRESIDENT,

Dear Mr. President: I suppose Herrick[236] has sent you the news through the Ordinary Diplomatic channels—as I instructed him to do—about the French Debt settlement. Now I do hate to trouble you so much about this again, for I think it has been up before you once or possibly twice before.

Well, Berengaria,[237] their trader, come back over here, and the settlement was received with general acclaim—by everybody that did-ent have to pay it. So as I write you this it looks like it will not be ratified by what they call the House of Deputies. Berengaria thought he had done pretty good. Everybody over here in public life that works out some financial scheme thinks he has done pretty good till they take their scheme to the House of Deputies. They are a nice agreeable bunch of fellows, but there is just something in them that won't let some man come in and talk money.

They are prefectly sane—for politicians. But the minute somebody mentions money or Stabilize the Franc, why, they are off life a prairie fire. Even Briand can't do anything with them. They have throwed him out so many times that he wears pads under his clothes. It seems that there is just some little minor difference or defect in the agreement with America. The change really don't mean anything, but they want to have it put just right before passing on it. There is just some three 000—naughts—on the end of some figures that they want to have erased. It was probably just a misprint, and taking off just those three little figures will of course make no material difference in the main settlement.

They stand by Berengaria's main settlement outside of, as I say, these three little minor defects. It's funny how they happen to notice them at all, a little thing like that, because they are usually very careless in such matters. So on this account we may not be able to close out this particular account quite as soon as I had lead you to believe. So I hope you dident hold Congress there all this time waiting. Of course some of them don't mind staying, for it will be their last trip. By-by.

Yours,

W. R.

Paris, France, June 26, '26.

Mr. President,

    White House,

My dear Mr. President: After all these weeks fixing and searching and plotting for you, I have at last found something that is really of some use, and it's the funniest thing where I found it—it was at Monte Carlo. Did you know—chances are you did on account of it being Monte Carlo—that that Casino, or gambling place, paid all the expenses of that entire Country and the owners prowled around in Yachts?

Well, I give it a very close study, and I have a scheme that I want to unfold to you that I think can be put into effect in Cuckooland. Now take, for instance, the District of Columbia, make it the Monaco of America. Now, of course, like in Monaco, the natives of the village are not allowed to play. Well, that same rule would hold good in the District of Columbia.

That would be no special hardship on residents of the District, as they are used to not having any privileges anyway. They just as well belong to Monaco as Columbia. They are not allowed to know

86

what it's all about, as it is now, so any reform no matter how terrible would be an aid to them. Instead of giving them Government positions—or Pensions, rather—as we do now, why, they could help take care of the Casino; in fact you could use most of the help that we have there now.

Another thing about this scheme of mine, it enables us to retain Mellon, that I know you are desirous of doing. Well, he could count up for us every night and take the statement to you, and every 6 months you could go before Congress and the Radio and read it— principally to the Radio.

Now if Monaco can support their entire little Country in luxury and yachts and no taxes at all just on what few Americans go over there, what could we do by having this right in Washington, where everybody could come and play without the inconvenience of a passport? Well, here is what I figure we would do. This is a very conservative estimate.

Now don't say it can't be done, because it is being done right in Wall Street, but we are not getting a cent out of it. No $100,000 for a seat to gamble in ours at Monte on the Potomac. Just come in and go to it.

And say, don't you think we wouldent take a big part of the play away from Wall Street. 'Course they would have one advantage of us down there. We would not be gambling in necessities or foods or anything like that. The outcome of ours would not affect anyone but the one gambling.

In other words, I am in favor of turning Washington from Red tape to Roulette. And here is what I figure conservatively would be your first six months' report. You walk right in and deliver the following:

"Gentlemen and Democrats, it gives me much pleasure to read to you the following financial report of the first six months of the new régime of financial Government, entitled, Betting for and by the People. I find that due to the dexterity of the little Ball dropping consecutively in the wrong pocket for the last six months, and the partial honesty of our Treasury, or adding up, Department, we find that we have won $6,395,826.10. The odd 10 cents, I might add, was wagered by Mr. Harry Lauder[238] on his this year's farewell tour.

"Now this sum accumulated by strict economy and mechanical methods in the past six months will enable us to reduce the taxes so low that we will have to pay some money to the taxpayers ourselves. We will not only feed and care for the residents of the District of Monaco here, but we will be able to get the more deserving of them a small yacht. In other words, we have what we think is a new idea in

87

Communistic Government. We are taking from the rich and distributing to the poor.

"On the continuation of the above platform I hereby offer myself for reëlection. In just four years more of a system like this we will have our Cars paid for and be able to pay cash for some small purchases, such as Chewing Gum and Pins and matches. And I hereby defy the Democratic Party to come out with anything in the way of a platform that equals mine in Economy to the masses.

"There is only one scheme that they could possibly come forward with that would raise more ready money than mine, but I don't think they dare put it forward. That would be the putting of a Tax on Murders, Robberies and Liquors, and all its subsidiaries. But I don't think they dare do that. You can't, in Politics, go against your Constituency.

"You, for instance, put a heavy tax on Liquor and you will find that it will do just like my able Confederate, Mr. Mellon, proved to you with the high Income tax rate—it will defeat its own purpose. They taxed Industry so high men wouldent engage in it, hence no revenue was received, and it is the same with Liquor—or anything else that sells under the name. People will resent it, and they will get even with you by not drinking it, and it will as my Mark Hanna[239] so aptly proved it in the tax question, defeat its own purpose.

"As for Crime and Robberies, that is carrying just as heavy a burden now as it possibly can. It looks like it was making a lot of money, but it's not. The business is overcrowded. Supply and demand regulate Robberies the same as it regulates anything else. The supply of people who have money to be robbed of will never exceed the demand to rob them. In other words, as soon as there is a man has a Dollar there is a robber to take it.

"But they will never stand a tax. When you pay your Lawyers, and have to retain them by the year, whether you are robbing or not, and then pay your Professional Bondsmen, and hand out hundreds among the various Police Forces, I tell you they don't have much left in the end. Statistics have proved—as I had my Attorney Sargent look them up for me—that very few of the present-day Criminals ever wind up with much. Then the late hours, and with the present price of Ammunition and the inconvenience of getting it, and Pistols—sometimes you have to walk a block—it just in the end figures out a fair living.

"So if the Democrats are so short-sighted as to claim a platform that will saddle a tax on Crime, they will absolutely kill the business. So, Ladies and Gentlemen, and you, too, Progressives, I think that the System as adopted by the great little Nation of Monaco—Monte Carlo

—with such great success for all these years—they have never a war or a Famine— this system as discovered and proposed by my able European accomplice, Mr. Rogers [cheers] has proved the Salvation of the whole of Cuckooland. The District of Columbia, as it was always formerly run, was a losing proposition. If we could have removed it with all that it contained years ago, we would today be on velvet. So that, Gentlemen, is the minutes of the last six months' Government and the program of the future. What is your pleasure?"

Now there would be some sense to a thing like that. People don't mind spending their money if they know it's not going for taxes.

Monaco has the right idea. Fix a Game where you are going to get it, but the fellow don't know you are getting it. A fellow can always get over losing money in a game of chance, but he seems so constituted that he can never get over money thrown away to a Government in Taxes. In other words, he will bet you on anything, but he won't pay it to you in Taxes.

Now lest Congressmen and Senators should feel some apprehension as to their future under a plan like this, I would like to state that they will be retained without having to face their Constituency—which I know is like going to a Dentist. The Senators will be the Croupiers, the ones that set there and rake in the Jack and place bets for the Tax Dodgers. And the custom is when a number wins straight up the winner is to tip the Croupiers. That would remind them of present conditions, when they put through a Bill lowering the tariff on something a constituent wants back home. The Congressmen, they would be the Hat-Check Boys.

This looks like the best bet over here. This Monaco is the only place I have been where everything is running Jake. There is no Government, there is nothing to interfere with anything or anybody; just that little old wheel rolling for them all the time.

I will keep looking, but this is going to be hard to beat.

Yours affectionately,

W. R.

Special Cable[240]

CALCOOL, *Whitehousewash:*

PARIS, June 26.—American dressmakers are making sketches of foreign dresses. American bootleggers are making sketches of foreign labels.

Yours for better labels,

WILLROG.

MR. PRESIDENT,
WHITE HOUSE.

My Dear Mr. President: Say, I wish you could get off sometime and come here. If you had the right kind of fellows there in your Cabinet you could get away. Other men get their business running so good that they come over here and travel around and see something, and it's funny to me that you, with the biggest business in the world, can't get men good enough that you can leave it for as long as you wanted to and go where you pleased. That shows right there that you havent got the right men.

Well, if you ever do accidentally stumble on anyone that you can leave there and trust, why, don't overlook this Spain. You know, not many Tourists or travelers get through here, because it's off the beaten track. Well, that is just what makes it good. Say, it's not only the most quaint country there is with lots to see, but it's the most productive from the soil standpoint of any one over here. It's the Oklahoma of Europe.

Well, I blew in here from down around Nice and Monte Carlo—one night—come in by way of Barcelona, a real thriving city and their principal seaport. Made a day trip into Madrid on as nice and comfortable a train as ever hauled you out of Washington. They are plowing in the old ways with Oxen and not even a plow, but a forked stick. But they sure are getting something raised. I tell you an oxen will raise as much as a Tractor if you don't use the tractor. Nobody hollering for Farm relief; every farmer was trying to make his own relief.[241]

Well, I found every Nation over there, whether they admitted it or not, was trying to dig up another Mussolini. Now between you and I, there are no more Mussolini's any more than there is more Calvin Coolidges. I am not handing you this just because I am over here on a mission for you, but it's the dead facts.

Well, I asked everybody, as they are all trying to dig up other Mussolini's, "Who has come the nearest to it?" Well, they all agreed that Spain had been fortunate enough to come nearer finding the right man than any of them—a man named Primo de Rivera.[242] France had been trying and they couldent tell whether they had one or not. They dident let one stay in long enough to find out if he could even spell Mussolini, much less act like him. England, when I first got to Europe, looked like they had a great fellow in this Baldwin. I went away and was gone 5 weeks, and when I got back he stood about like an impeached Governor.

They make 'em or break 'em quick over here. You don't get any four years' trial like you-all do over home, and then we have to put up with the regardless. A Premier never unpacks his grip over here. He just engages his room by the day. Portugal, the week I was in Madrid, had three Revolutions and 4 changes of Government in one day, and they havent got daylight saving either, or else they could have squeezed in another Revolution. Germany was in a Panic, Greece was changing leaders oftener than they did their shirts, Turkey had dug up a new one.

So I said, "Well, will you tell me who has lasted at least a week?"

So I found that this Primo de Rivera had been in for over two years. Now that over here would be about the same as you staying in for life. In Seniority he comes next to Mussolini. So I says to myself, Will, I know Calvin will want me to go see him and get some dope on his system. I had a letter from the main one of our help in Rome, Mr. Fletcher, who by the way is an awful good man; and if you can ever throw anything his way, why, you can bet it will be taken care of in a Business and Diplomatic way—a rare combination.

Well, I go around to see our Help here in Madrid. His name is Mr. Ogden Hammond,[243] and, as you know, he is a regular fellow. I don't know when I have met anyone that was more amiable and charming. You know, you kinder got to watch out about Spain, Mr. President, in your appointments of Ambassadors. Spain maintains a lot of dignity, and you not only have to send a good level-headed business man but you have to have a man that can really, he and his wife, uphold the social and dignified end. I think more so than some of these other Nations, because they take it pretty serious in Spain.

Now Mr. Hammond is new in the Diplomatic game, but he is certainly making good, and they like him. You see, you either got to be one or the other with people like these. You got to show some dignity or not any at all. That's how My old Friend Aleck Moore[244] was; they liked him. Aleck just went into Spain the same as he would go into Pittsburgh. He knew how they acted there. If anybody had any dignity, they wouldent be in Pittsburgh. So Aleck just acted natural and they fell for it. This fellow Hammond is used to dignity; he acts natural and they fell for it. Well, Aleck made them and us a good man. He made good in every way, and what's amusing about it is you taking him away and then he turns around and nominates Vare. Well, he was just What Spain needed—a little lightening up. You see, through their close connection with the English, they have kinder sorter grabbed off part of England's allaged dignity too. Soo a little Pittsburgh Society mixed in sorter brought them back to earth again.

This Hammond has a lovely family, and they are just in their new Embassy Building, and it shows up pretty good. 'Course we always have the poorest-looking ones of anybody, but this one in Madrid now is one we don't have to feel ashamed of. Well, Mr. Hammond wanted to know if I wanted to see this Primo de Rivera, and I answering in the affirmative, he arranged for me to call at the Premier's office the next day and he would grant me an interview.

Well, Mr. Hammond was so nice he even went down with me, and also Mr. Cunningham,[245] our Commercial Attaché; a very good man; just an old smart Country boy from Texas, but he knows his stuff. Held the job 6 years and sure does savvy the language. Well, he was kind enough to go along as Interpreter. This Mr. Hammond don't speak a bad Spanish himself, by the way.

This Rivera was an Army man all his life, and he has had a lot to do with winding up this Morrocan affair. He is the first one that told Spain what to do down there, and they took his advice, caught old Abd-el Krim, give him to France, and now France don't know what to do with him; so Spain is even with France. His Secretary spoke excellent English—that is, as well as I know what Excellent English is. English is more spoken in Spain among the Royalty—and people of what is foolishly spoken of all over the world as Breeding—than any other nation. All the highly educated ones speak English in preference to Frénch. But that's the trouble with traveling in Spain. The high-ups all speak English, but nobody else. So you are stuck. How are you going to get to the high-ups?

I knew about a dozen words of what I had always been led to believe were Spanish, and Bill, Jr., had taken it at School. So I thought I was going in pretty well fortified. Well, Bill either had a bad Teacher or else he was the worst Spanish scholar in the world; and these 12 words of mine in the whole 8 days with constant trying every chance I got, I never found a one that would fit. They might have been Spanish in Oklahoma, but they were Russian in Madrid. I stabbed in Spanish one morning at breakfast for what I thought was Strawberries and drew Lettuce Salad. I am going to take those few words I know of back to the fellow I got them from and hand them back marked Not Used.

But you can always live in foreign Countries, for they have a fellow in every Hotel in Europe called the Concierge, and I want to tell you that they are perfectly at home with an Eskimo. They can tend to more things and talk more languages than any people I ever saw.

But I must get back to my interview with this Leader of Spain. There was an awful lot of Army Officers outside in the Anteroom; they dident know, I suppose, but what I had been sent there by Ibanez.[246] Well, this Rivera got up and come and met us. He was in

92

military Uniform, and had on quite a few Medals. I wouldent say that he was overdressed with them, but he was just on the border of what one would call good taste in medal dressing.

I complimented him on the condition of his country, because I could say nothing less and be truthful, for Spain is really in very excellent shape. Its money is at a staple price—in fact going up. He told me that he was just now getting things along the lines he wanted them. He said he wished that we allowed more trade with them, as they were our greatest buyers. They do buy more from us than they buy from any other Nation. It runs away in the hundreds of millions, and he seemed to think it rather unfair that our high tariff totally excluded some things, like Grapes. They used to ship millions of dollars' worth of table grapes in, and all at once somebody said there was a bug in one of them, and they just stopped off, and now they don't allow a one in there. Well, he dident think that was hardly fair.

The League of Nations conference was on just at that time and I asked him how they felt about it, for I knew that Spain and Brazil[247] had caused quite a row at the other meeting. Well, he thought that as Spain was the largest individual Neutral during the last war, they would be allowed into a Peace Conference to prevent wars. But they had not been given a permanent seat, and he would not allow them to just be in there as a temporary member to be kicked out when somebody liked. So I told him that the reason that they wouldent let them in was that they were not ready for a war. That's the reason why they wouldent let Germany in at first; she was in no shape for a war.

Now between you and I, Calvin, I have talked to everybody that I could possibly get to that I could understand in this whole trip, and they all feel the same about this League and Disarming and World Courts and all that stuff. They feel like England and France runs the whole thing and they don't want anything to do with it.

Between you and I, there ain't any of them got any use for the other one, and you can't blame 'em for looking out after themselves. Say, you give them as much ocean on each side of them as we have, and then on the other two ends a Mexico and a Canada, they might start talking some disarming with you too.[248] There is a lot of things talk good in a speech, but you come to working it out when you are up against hundreds of years of previous wars and hatreds, they don't pan out.

I had been to the attempted Disarmament Conference at Geneva and had heard his Delegation speak, so I asked him about Disarmament. I got the same laugh out of him I had out of Mussolini. He had the usual European reply: "When everybody else disarms, I will disarm."

Rivera had been asked to go to America, to the Philadelphia Sesqui-Centanial, and I took it upon myself to extend an additional invitation. I knew it would be all right with Mayor Kendrick,[249] as I knew him before he met Butler.[250] In fact I knew Kendrick when he was nothing but a Shriner. I knew he would be glad if I dug him up another customer.

Well, this fellow would really like to go, and he asked about Aleck—said he would have to go see him. You know, Spain spent a great lot of money and sent over a very fine exhibit, and if he comes over there you will see quite a fellow. He is not the live go-get-'em-knock-'em-down-kid like Mussolini, but he gets some of the same things done in a quieter way. He has Spain working and producing. He touched a button and I thought maby he was going to give me a Picture, but instead come a man with a tray. Well, that looked like some real fellowship.

He said, "It's not much; it won't interfere with you Gentlemen's Prohibition obligation—it's just a little sherry wine."

I am not much up on wines. I wouldent know Sherry from White Mule, but I am going to take out a small stack on this one. Well, Hammond, who has always been used to good stuff, and Cunningham, who speaks and drinks the language perfectly, why, they said this was marvelous. Then he explained to us that it was some stuff that Queen Isabella, I believe it was, had put these few bottles away for Columbus when he come in from a hard trip exploring. It was supposed to have some kind of spices in it, they said. I slipped my glass over to be re-loaded. I says if I can just inveigle this old General out of a couple of more jolts of this Discovery medicine I will go out and hide America where no one can find it.

Now it wasent so much the good Sherry, but it was the hospitality of the thing; it was being so thoughtful. And that is the atmosphere that you will find that permeates the whole of Spain. They are glad to see you and they show that they are glad.

I never got a thing out of Mussolini. The Prince of Wales offered me a Cigarette, but he knew I dident smoke. So the Premier of Spain is the headliner in the hospitality race.

He said, "Anything I can do for you in Spain?" I thanked him and told him how nice that was; for I knew if there was anything in Spain that I did ask for, he was the only one that could get it. I told him if he even went to Philadelphia, why, to let me know and I would give him a letter to Connie Mack and Artie Fletcher[251] and they would show him the town.

Well, we just had a pleasant and mighty fine visit, and I felt like I had been honored by seeing and talking too a very capable man—

94

perhaps the best that Spain has produced in a long time. Mr. Hammond was very pleased with the visit and said that that was the most he had heard him talk and discuss things with anyone.

The next morning at my Hotel I received the following letter. He sent two copies, one in Spanish and this one with the English Translation. Both were autographed by him. Well, that was a mighty thoughtful thing to do, and I would like to have you, Mr. President, pass this along to somewhere in Philadelphia, to show them that there is a very big man that knows of Philadelphia.

Also show Mr. Kellogg that all our help bear very friendly relations with these people, and if the chance comes to slip 'em a raise, *why*, to do it.

[Insert the letter, and get it in there before that Dam fair is over.]

PRESIDENCIA
    DEL
CONSEJO DE MINISTROS

WILL ROGERS, ESQ.
HOTEL RITZ.

Dear Sir: I beg to say that I have been so pleased with your visit this morning and so touched by the cordiality of your expressions toward Spain, in which I reciprocate with the highest esteem toward the United States, that I come to pray you kindly to be the bearer of my personal message full of hearty wishes to the great country which is yours and whose courageous and wonder-working character is held by all Spaniards in great admiration.

I feel flattered to know that my country is more and more appreciated in the United States every day, but I am sure this appreciation will become far greater when your countrymen become better acquainted with Spain as it is today—a cultivated, working, peaceful and disciplined country.

Spain has become a good client of the United States, and I long to see your country reciprocating with mine under this economical point of view, instead of creating some difficulties to the import of Spanish goods.

We feel delighted to be officially represented in the approaching great Exhibition of Philadelphia and wish and hope that the Spanish pavilion, though a modest one, may be the expression of our character and historical traditions, well meaning that it is Spain's wish to be present in future wherever there may be any celebration meaning peace, art and work.

I desire to the great American nation all blessings from above and all prosperities on earth.

Sincerely yours,
PRIMO DE RIVERA.

You might not know it, but this fellow as a Dictator has even Mussolini beat. Mussolini has got a Congress, or House of Deputies. But when this fellow come in they threw the whole Gang out. There is no more Spanish Senate or Deputies. They are renting out their rooms for a Bullfight. This Gentleman runs the whole thing. The King calls up and asks what costume to wear that day.

Oh, yes, I asked him about the Bullfight. I had been to one two days before. I dident want to go; I knew I wouldent like it; then I thought, well I better go and see it; that's the only way I can learn just what it is, and by me not going is not going to save any horse's life. I debated up to the last minute. I went, but I wouldent let Bill go. I knew he would be broken up over it, for he is a horse kid from his heart.

Some other time I will explain the whole thing to you; but to get this letter over and off to you before another Cabinet meeting I will say that I watched up to a certain time, when I ducked my head down behind the concrete wall, as we were in the first row. A very nice Spanish Chap[252] who I had met in New York was my Host, and he would tell me when to look up again. I am a pretty tough egg, but I couldent go that Horse business.

There has been a lot of agitation in government circles as to doing away with the killing of the horses, so I asked Primo de Rivera. He said that they were trying to Legislate now against it. He dident like it. I never met any of the Spaniards that did. It is done to weaken the Bull. The Bull-fighters claim that it is almost impossible, or at least would take too long to kill the bull if he was not tired out and his neck weakened by the tossing around of old blindfolded Horses. If that was done I think that it could perhaps be made much better and especially if they dident kill the bull either, for all their best work is done before the Bull is killed. The actual killing is a mere detail.

I don't want to go to a Country and then Criticize their Sport— every Nation to its own way of enjoying themselves. We are mixing in enough things without telling somebody else how to spend their spare time. It's all in what you are brought up to and are used to, and I want to dispel a theory you often hear by foreigners to Spain, and that is that the Bull hasent got a chance, the men have all the best of it. Yes, they do; that's a fact, as the Bull is always killed by someone.

96

But don't tell me about that old No-danger thing. Three men were carried out the afternoon I was there; one of them twice. They would carry him out and he would come to and would crawl back in again. None of these were seriously hurt, but all were caught; and the Sunday I dident go—thank goodness—Monte[253] was killed right there in Madrid.

He was one of their Topnotchers. He was practically killed right in the ring, So forget that old Gag that there is no danger. So I told him I certainly hoped they would fix it up some way to at least do away with the horse business.

Over in New York, at the International Polo games, I had met the Party of Spaniards who come over. Among them was the Duke of Alba.[254] He is the most Royal person in Spain—more than the King, for his comes both sides of the house. He is a mighty fine Democratic kind of a fellow, educated in England and is part English. He asked me to his Palace. Well, I had seen these Dukes' Palaces all over Italy and Spain and around and been in them as Curio places. They would show you where the Dukes lived. So I was glad and I told him so when he called me up—that I sure did want to see a Palace with a live Duke in it.

Say, it wasent overrated any. His people are descendants of Columbus and he showed me 24 of Columbus' letters and old maps. Asked me to the Polo game the next day and said he would have me meet the King, as he was playing. I told him I thought I could arrange it so maby I could be out there.

Well, Bill, Jr., and I went out and we met him and had a fine chat with him before the game started. He is a very pleasant, good-natured kind of a fellow, just like we have always heard he was. I took off my hat when I was introduced and was standing there holding it and he said, "Put on your hat." Well, on account of the King commanding me, why, of course I did. We talked about Polo. He said there wouldent be much of a Game, as all their best players were in England playing. He wanted to know how I liked Spain, and how long I was going to stay. He dident act or look any more like a King than anything. He said he had heard I was quite a Rope thrower. That would have been a laugh among good Ropers. He spoke very good English—in fact almost as good as me. He is very tall and very wiry built. He went on in to dress for the game they were going to play for a set of Cups.

Well, they started, and I thought it was bad form not to let the king beat at anything. But say a King dident mean anything to that Gang. They rode him off the Ball, they run into him, they bumped him, and he was giving as well as taking. There was times there when

97

it dident look like there was going to be any more Royalty left than a Rabbit. He played back on his side, and he is a very good player; I think that he is rated at 6 Goals. Well, you are up in the Big League when you can carry six Goals. But here is the Joke of the whole thing—everybody outrun him; there was a lot better horses in the game than he had.

Say, listen, if I was King of some Country and we was having a Polo game, I want to tell the world that William would prance out astride the best steeds that entered the Arena that day. If some Guy outrun me he wouldent do it but once. I would issue a Kingly decree then and there that he dismount, and if necessary I would chop his bean off just to get his old filly. No, sir, if I was in the King business they might outplay me, but they sure wouldent have me outmounted. Why, he was on a lot of old Dogs about like some of mine. But you could tell he was there. Same way with the Prince of Wales— he had a pack of Hounds for his Polo string.

Shoot! What's the use being King or Prince or something! I would show 'em who was Daddy. All he got that day was beat. After they finished, there was another game. But he went in and dressed, and after he come out, he and the Duke of Alba they come by where Bill and I was watching the other game.

He apologized for his side's poor game. I hadent seen anything poor about it outside of getting beat.

He must have a kind of a sense of Humor, because he said, "My forwards layed down; they dident do a thing." Well, that's the usual alibi of a back. If I had talked with one of them I guess he would have said, "If that King Guy had played up to his game, we would have beat."

He said he was going to England the next week to play. He shook hands with us again and said he was rushing over to a race meet where he had to present the cup to the winner in an Army race. He seemed glad that we liked Spain and said that he was going to try to come to America some time—perhaps during the next International Polo match. The Queen was sitting in front of the Clubhouse watching the game. She is very pretty and a very big favorite, as she does an immense lot of charity work.

A few days before Bill and I had been on a sight-seeing tour and they took us through the King's Stables. Well, sir, here was this barn about the size of the Pennsylvania Hotel in New York, and all these fine stalls, and here who do I see but a lot of old mules standing back in those fine stalls.

I said to the guide, "What are these Hard-Tails doing parked in here?"

He said, "Why, they are American Mules, they use them here to drive to the Carriages to take the Servants home from the Palace." The Stable was right by the Palace. Well, they looked so natural I wanted to go in and kiss one. Here was St. Joe, Missouri, Boonville and Sedalia right under my nose. Here we are, I thought, Me and the Mules, over here in the King's Stable and one of us is just as much out of place as the other. But it kinder made me feel good to be among my own people. Now here they were, about 25 or 30 of them, great big old fellows. They would hitch them to the old-time closed carriages and take the Servants home.

I says, "Why, don't they use a flivver?" For there is, by the way, more American Cars in Spain than any Country in Europe.

He told me: "They won't go in an Automobile. That's the way they always come and that's the way they are always going to come."

We went from there into the Garage. There was every kind of car in there from a pair of Roller Skates to an Aeroplane. This King is a kind of a speed Bug, and they have Secret service men that follow him in a car and he is always trying to get cars that will outrun them. They just got a new one now since he did. They will run over him if he don't get out of their way now.

Then they have a room where there is the old State Carriages, for hundreds of years back, of all the different Kings and Queens. He showed us a black one and said, "That was Queen Isabella's. [I think that's the one. It was the one that backed Columbus, whichever one that was]. Well, he said, "She was sorter queer—that hearse-looking one belonged to her—she was rather odd; she pawned her jewels, that was hers."

I said, "Yes, She was considered Queer, and all she did was discover America. What did these others ever find that wasent queer?"

They had one there that followed the one that the King rides in. In case something happens to it, why, he is supposed to get out and get in this next one. I don't know why they think something is going to happen in one day after they have lasted all these hundreds of years; and it looks like somebody would let them get in with them if his broke down. But you cant figure out this Royalty. They have one way of doing a thing and they will lose a leg before they will change it. I looked up toward the palace but the barn was as near as I could get to it. But I was like the Mules—I was tickled to get in the barn.

Madrid is a mighty pretty place. You will see the time soon when there will be a tremendous Tourist travel to Spain. But you sure want to get ready to change your hours. Shows start in the Theaters at night at a quarter of eleven, and then nobody comes in till the second act, about 12 o'clock. Dinner is never before 9:30 or 10 o'clock at night.

The most miserable and lonesome half day I ever spent in my life was one morning in Madrid. I got up at 8:30 and went out on the street. Well, from then to noon I had Madrid entirely to myself. They commenced piling out for Coffee about eleven. That don't mean the working people don't work; they do. You will see them going to it at night in the fields and in the city up to and after nine oclock.

I just wish, as I told you before, Calvin, that you could get over here. If this Rivera comes over there I will give him a letter to you, and don't fail to see him, for he is an awful nice chap. I wish you had been with me in there and seen those old Mules.

Well, I must get on to France, as Briand resigns again tomorrow. If I don't see him resign tomorrow I will have to wait over two more days before he resigns again. Will incidentally drop in on this Herrick, our help there, and see what he is doing. If he turns out as well as these others, why, we will have no cause for worry. For all these Boys in every Country I have been in are doing fine. 'Course none of them have anything to do, but they are doing it good. You know, that's the hardest thing in the world—to do nothing good. But they are nice kids all of them, and I hope you don't bring any of them home. Remember what Aleck did with Vare.

If Paris don't get me, you will hear again, soon .

Yours devotedly,

WILL.

Special Cable[255]

CALCOOL, *Washhousewhite:*

LONDON, July 30.—Mellon is escaping through France, trying to reach the Italian border to go under the protection of Mussolini.[256]

Yours,

WILLROG.

Special Cable

CALCOOL, *Whitewashhouse:*

LONDON, August 2.—A bunch of American Tourists were hissed and stoned yesterday in France, but not until they had finished buying.

Yours,

WILLROG.

CALCOOL, *Whitehousewash:*

LONDON, August 3.—When Borah asked England and France what had become of that 400,000,000 acres of land they divided up after the war, that stopped all debt arguments over here. He is always thinking up some question nobody can answer. He even sticks you.

Suzanne Lenglen[257] has been landed by Pyle.[258] He is now here in London trying to get Bernard Shaw[259] to turn professional and write for money.

Regards to "Cuckooland,"

WILLROG.

Special Cable

CALCOOL, *Washhousewhite:*

LONDON, August 4.—England's House of Parliament, or Commons rather (I have seen it and prefer calling it the Commons), closed today to give some of the lady members a chance to try and swim the English Channel.[260]

I wanted to have my wife try it, but the Channel is all booked up for the next month.

Churchill, in his closing remarks, still says[261] "We borrowed the money, but we don't owe it."

Yours aquatically,

WILLROG.

Special Cable

CALCOOL, *Whitehousewash:*

LONDON, August 6.—General Andrews, our prohibition director, is here and has just held a meeting with the British shippers to eliminate any delay in getting it in.[262]

Yours,

WILLROG.

Special Cable

CALCOOL, *Whitehousewash:*

LONDON, August 7.[263]—Mellon in Italy to find out for you how Mussolini stands with everybody.

Yours respectfully,

WILLROG.

101

Special Cable

Calcool, *Whitewashhouse:*

London, August 8.—Hordes of other Channel swimmers are leaving for their respective homes. If they will only go to work when they get there Gertrude Ederle[264] will have accomplished much more than her original feat.

England is trying to get in on the credit of it. They claim they furnished the land for her to land on, otherwise she would never have made it. France can't get any ad out of it at all, outside of being a good place to start somewhere from.

Yours truly,

Willrog.

Special Cable

Calcool, *Whitehousewash:*

London, August 9.—I had this debt thing about quieted down when this old fellow Clemenceau[265] broke out. I can't be everywhere.

I think any man over eighty or under sixty should be barred from expressing an opinion on debts.   Yours,

Willrog.

Special Cable

Calcool, *Whitewashhouse:*

London, August 10.—It is open season now in Europe for grouse and Americans.

They shoot the grouse and put them out of their misery.

Yours truly,

Willrog.

Special Cable

Calcool, *Whitewashhouse:*

London, August 11.—I told you how bad it's getting with the tourists over here.[266]

Some of them are getting almost what they deserve.

Yours informally,

Willrog.

102

Special Cable

CALCOOL, *Washhousewhite:*

LONDON, August 12.—I had a long talk with friend Barney Baruch. He did not dictate that letter Clemenceau wrote—he only gave him the idea of it.

Baruch has gone to shoot grouse.

He names them after the Republicans and has never missed one.

Yours for information,

WILLROG.

Special Cable

CALCOOL, *Whitehousewash:*

LONDON, August 16.—England had an earthquake yesterday[267] and their newspapers didn't know enough to call it a fire. What are you going to do with people like that?

P.S.—There is a cricket match going on here that has been on for three months— one game.[268] The earthquake didn't even wake up the spectators.

Yours observingly,

WILLROG.

Special Cable

CALCOOL, *Washhousewhite:*

LONDON, August 17.—The King[269] is in Scotland, and it certainly is lonesome here.

The same cricket game that I told you about before is still going on. One man has been batting three days.

The score is now 800 runs to 500 and Australia has only been at bat once.

Come over and see it. If the tea holds out, it will run till Winter.

I have been thrown out of the grounds twice for applauding. They contend I was a boisterous element.

Yours for long, lingering sportsmanship.

WILLROG.

Special Cable

CALCOOL, *Washhousewhite:*

LONDON, August 18.—Secretary of State Kellogg spoke last night in Plattsburg on disarmament.[270] It is a good idea for Plattsburg and even Chicago and New York, but our delegation starved to death trying to get somebody interested in it at Geneva this summer.

Yours for preparedness,

WILLROG.

Special Cable

CALCOOL, *Washhousewhite:*

LONDON, August 20.—You refuse to give Philippines their complete independence.[271] I am with you. Why should the Philippines have more than we do?

Yours for 100 per cent. freedom for everybody, including Ireland.

WILLROG.[272]

Special Cable

CALCOOL, *Whitehousewash:*

LONDON, August 22.—One of the quietest weeks over here in months—nobody wrote an open letter to you, nobody swam the channel; in fact, not even a single European dictator was shot at. Can it be the League is working?

Yours for truth, even if it interferes with news,

WILLROG.

Special Cable

CALCOOL, *Whitewashhouse:*

LONDON, August 23.—Biggest news over the week-end was an amateur dictator found escaping by wireless in Greece, and a baby hippotamus was born at the London zoo.[273] Of the two events the last was the biggest and of more interest to humanity. Baby hippos are rare, but alleged dictators are lurking in every cafe in Europe. Mussolini has had more bad imitators of him than even Georgie Cohan.[274]

Yours for a better class of dictators.

WILLROG.

Special Cable

CALCOOL, *Whitehousewash:*

LONDON, August 24.—Parliament, which had adjourned, has just today called a special session within a few days. If we ever did a thing like that in the Summer we would have to hold it in Europe or out on a Chautauqua circuit,[275] so we could get a few members present. Queer people, these English legislators. They are satisfied to stay in their own country; in fact, they rather like it.

Yours for constant public service,

WILLROG.

Special Cable

CALCOOL, *Whitewashhouse:*

LONDON, August 25.—France is very quiet. The rise in taxes was only proposed. Deer season opened in Scotland for all those who can't hit grouse. Debts and dictators quiet today.

Yours editorially,

WILLROG.

THIS letter is addressed to His Majesty the President of the northern part of the United States, including parts of Ohio, and sent to the fish hatchery of the state of New York, at White Pines.

DUBLIN, Ireland, late in August, in the year '26, during the reign of President Cosgrave.[276]

My Dear Mr. President—if I may call you dear without raising the enmity of too many of the qualified voters of Cuckooland: I havent written you for some time. I knew you were busy fishing and worrying with Al Smith, so I had enough consideration for your feelings not to bother you even with a few trifles such as our Foreign Policy. I heard about the Fish you caught and sold to the Museum. Keep the old Economy measures going as long as it will last. I am glad you invited Al up there to the camp, because there is nothing that shows to the world what a polyglot nation America is more than the mingling of the East Side of New York and the west side of Vermont.

Al is a good boy and the longer you know him the better you will like him. You and Al kinder put me in mind of each other. 'Course, you are up earlier in the morning, but he is up later at night. Al can stay awake till twelve o'clock and never bat an eye.

Well, I guess by the time this reaches you, you will have brushed all the Chiggers and Fleas and Mosquitoes off of you, and are back in the White House with nothing to worry you but Farmers and Democrats. If it had been me, President, I believe I would have stayed up there all year.

And by the way, while you were picking out places to spend a summer vacation, did you ever receive a communication from the Commercial Club of Claremont, Oklahoma? I told them to write you and I gave them your address. They just lost it, that's about what happened.

Well, if you think you can ever stand another vacation, why, there is a part of the Country that I would like to see you get interested in. There is nobody got a Camp there, but everybody has houses. We havent got any Wall-eyed Pike, but we got some of the best Buffalo Catfish in the world in the Verdigris River. I will stake you to my place right where I was born, just twelve miles out of Claremore. It's just run down and old enough that it will remind you of Vermont. I will get a special dispensation from the authorities of Rogers County, so they won't bother you, because you will be the first Republican that ever slept in the House, and I will have to fix the Game Laws for protection. It's a typical White House, for I Just had it whitewashed two years ago, figuring on John W. Davis[277] taking it. But owing to circumstances over which he had no control, why, that fell through.

Now I will enumerate a few of the advantages that Oklahoma, and especially Claremore, hold over the rest of the United States. In the first place you will be bothered by no Governors. If Trapp[278] or his successor, either one, try to get in, I have a sign up on the bob-wire gate at the section line: Nothing Allowed in That Will Interfere With the Work or Scare the Animals. So you won't bee obliged to be nise to anybody for courtesy's sake; and then, too, you won't be bothered with Politicians. Oklahoma is so far away that a Politician can't pay his way that far. Nobody can afford the trip but a Statesman, and the road from town out is so bad that even he will get discouraged before he gets there, and turn around and go back.

Now I am not located on a bootlegging route from Canada. The best you can get there is just home-talent stuff. But the Boys have had a lot of practice making it, for Oklahoma has always been dry—certainly I am laughing. What did you think I was doing?—and on account of our years of experience I don't want it to be considered in the nature of egotism, but they do say we build it better than anybody. I can show you stills there 100 years old. It's a tradition with us; it's not a get-rich-quick industry. We take pride in the quality, not the price.

Now if this description interests you in the way of a summer place, why, I can have it fixed so you won't have to come through St. Louis on the way out, which is an inducement. If you decide to take it, I wish you would either take it this summer or next summer. I wouldent like to make any deal with you on it later than '28.

Now I hate to inject any business of a personal nature into any of our communications, but what I have suggested above is for the good of all concerned; for you must realize that Oklahoma is a doubtful State in the next election, the same as New York is.

Well, I will stop and get this off; I want to have it catch the boat.

Will drop you a line in a couple more days if I have nothing else to do.

Watch the farmers with half of one eye, Lowden with the other half and Borah with the entire remaining other eye.

Your little "cottage" in Europe,

WILLIE ROGERS.

Special Cable

CALCOOL, *Whitewashhouse:*

DUBLIN, August 25.[279]—Am bringing family greetings from Dublin to every man on the force.

WILLROG.

Special Cable

CALCOOL, *Washhousewhite:*

CORK, August 26.[280]—I have been in twenty countries and the only one where American tourists are welcomed wholeheartedly by everybody is Ireland. And the funny part about it is there is more to see there than in all the others put together. They don't owe us and they dont hate us. The Lakes of Killarney is where Switzerland got their idea of lakes. Ireland is a friend of everybody, even England. This endorsement is on the level and calls for no appointment from Tammany Hall[281] whatever.

Yours imploringly,

WILLROG.

CORK, Ireland, August 26.

PRESIDENT COOLIDGE,

Dear Mr. Coolidge:[282] Well, I have been gathering up a lot of facts and I am just about in shape to report. I have the biggest news for you that I have had since I have been your little Shack in Europe. You know, of course, or perhaps you have had it hinted to you, that we stand in Europe about like a Horse Thief. Now I want to report to you that that is not so. It is what you call at Amherst, "erroneous." We don't stand like a Horse Thief abroad. Whoever told you we did is flattering us. We don't stand as good as a Horse Thief. They knew what you were sore at them for.

107

Now I have been in all kinds of Countries—about all they have over here, if somebody don't come along with self-determination for small nations and carve out a couple of dozen more. But I have looked them all over. Now you will have people coming back over there tell you that it is not so that we are in bad.

They get their information from people who are trying to be polite to them. But you just get to talking and let an argument start, and you will mighty soon see the old feeling crop out.

But here is what I want to write you about, and the thing that you never hear mentioned or even thought of. Everybody talks about how we are hated—it is to conversation in Europe what Prohibition has been at home. Well, when the discussion would gradually come to the Shylocks, as we had been christened, why, I would just casually, of course, admit that we were a band of highbinders, and were just waiting to get England or France up a back alley and knock 'em in the head and get what little they had left; and while they were discussing jubilantly the subject of our unpopularity I would, in order to keep up the conversation and not change the subject, just nonchalantly remark, "Will you enumerate to me, in their natural order, the number of Nations that you people can call bosom friends?"

Well, they had never thought of that; but when you insist on a count, he finds that he not only could enumerate them on his fingers but he could count them on his fingers if he had been unfortunate enough to have both arms off.

These Guys over here are so busy celebrating our unpopularity that they don't stop to look around to see how they stand themselves. So don't let them stampede you, Cal, with our unpopularity. We have become so unpopular that we are as bad off as every other Nation. If you can find me one Nation in Europe that has a real down-to-earth, sincere regard for any other Nation, I will jump out of the top of the Washington Manument and see if Jackie Coogan can catch me as I fall.

I have purposely looked for combinations that were friendly toward each other, and I have yet to find any two that wasent at heart ready to pounce on each other if they thought they could get away with it—unless it was Latvia up toward the Arctic Ocean and Madagascar down in the Indian Ocean. They, perhaps, have no particular grievance against each other, but they will have as soon as they find out where each other are.

France and England think just as much of each other as two rival bands of Chicago Bootleggers. Gloating over our unpopularity is the only thing they have ever agreed on perfectly. Just by the luck of the draw they happened to be paired together in the last war, but they been fighting each other for over a thousand years. Waterloo will be remembered longer than any debt. Italy went to bat on the side of France in the last Series, but that was just because Austria was on the opposite side. If it hadent been for that, they would have just pitched up a dollar to see what side to go in on. A Frenchman and an Italian love each other just about like Minneapolis and St. Paul. Spain and France have the same regard for each other as Fort Worth and Dallas.

Spain feels that they fought the Riffs for four years and then France come in and got all the best land at the settlement.

Russia hates everybody so bad it would take her a week to pick out the one she hates most. Poland is rarin' to fight somebody so bad that they just get up and punch themselves in the jaw. They can't make up their minds whether to jump on Russia, Germany, or go up and annex Lithuania. Turkey has been laying off three months now without any war, and Peace is just killing them. You can't even pass out of the south of Russia into Rumania. Bulgaria is feeding an Army and deriving no benefits from it whatever.

Greece has some open time that they are trying to fill in. They will take on anybody but Turkey; they are about cured of them. Czecho-Slovakia is a new country, and they feel that a war would just about give them the proper prestige and tradition that a Nation should have in future to point to. Japan is filling up Chinese Manchuria with Japs and copping it away from China so fast that Russian interests are menaced there; and Russia is doing all they can to populate that end of Russia with Emigrants, for they know that sooner or later these two will have to tangle.

Mussolini is raising five hundred thousand children every year, and needs somewhere to stake 'em out. He will have to have somewhere sometime, but Nations are so civilized nowadays that they won't think of selling each other land like individuals do. No, they must be made to go out and fight for it. France and England have enough colonies that they could sell Italy, on long-term payments, all the land she would ever need, and besides, make an alliance with her in the bargain; but no, that's not done. Once you get a piece of land you must hang onto it whether you use it or not. So that means Italy sooner or later has got to go out and fight for it. They won't do it now because this Guy is too wise, but he will when he thinks they are ready.

Portugal would like to join somebody in a war just to make them forget their own troubles. Holland just sets there and greases her windmills and sells butter and eggs and cheese to the Kaiser. Norway, Sweden and Denmark are apparently getting on pretty good; but you call a Swede a Dane, or get any of the three of them mixed up, and you better reach for your hat.

Germany, the winner of the last war, is about the only one that is not looking for trouble. When the Allies took their Army and Navy away from them, shortsighted Statesmen dident know it, but they did them the greatest favor that was ever done a Nation. It dident leave them a thing to do but go to work. Their Reparations cost them less than France and England spend on their Officers' uniforms. So Germany is just sitting pretty. Austria is just like a joint snake that somebody cuts up in pieces; it will take itself till sundown to get gathered up and see how much it has left.

Germany, the winner of the last war, is about the only one that is not looking for trouble.

Diplomats are just running around in circles over here, trying to get together and draw up different treaties and compacts. You hear people get up and talk about the sentiment and the comradeship that was formed during the war, and how it will never be forgotten. Why, the war has only been over a few years, and you see how much credit each one gives the other for helping. Everybody thinks everybody else dident do anything.

It looks to me like the last war ought to be the greatest example against any future wars. What I mean by that is the winners are the losers. I have been in every Nation that was humorously supposed to have won the war, and then last I visited Germany, which is humorously referred to as the loser, and I want to tell you that if the next

110

war is to be anything like the last one I wouldent give you a five-cent piece to win it. Wars strike me as being the only game in the world where there is absolutely no winner—everybody loses.

But you can't make these people believe that. They go in great for tradition over here, and if a thing has been happening for years, why, there is no reason why it should not keep on happening. That's why these Disarmment Conferences never get anywhere. I went down to Geneva to see the so-called Preliminary Disarmament Conference, and I stayed till they were throwing inkstands at each other.[283] We do more hollering about it than anybody, but you just put ourselves in some of these European Nations' places, surrounded by maybe three or four Nations that are as strong or maybe stronger than we are, and you would see how much we would be yapping about disarmament.

You let France change places with Canada, and Germany change places with Mexico, and England with Cuba, and Japan with Hawaii, and you would see if we would be so anxious to disarm. Say, If I dident have any more friends than some of these Nations have around them, I not only would not disarm but I would get another Gun, and wouldent only have a gun in each hand as I went to bed but I wouldent go to bed—I would stay up and watch all night.

The way we look at things, we think Alsace-Lorraine was the only Country that was ever taken away from another Nation. Why, you can't find a piece of ground in Europe that hasent been taken at least a dozen times from somebody or other that really think they have an original claim to it. Italy wants Nice and the Mediterranean Coast back just as bad as France wanted Alsace-Lorraine, and they say that now that France has it back they have succeeded in doing something that was never known in the history of the Country. In the old days Alsace-Lorraine under Germany had two parties—one was for Germany and the other one was against whatever the first one was for. No matter what it was, it was known that they never agreed on anything. But now that France has it they are both united; they both have it in for France. That was more than Germany could ever do to combine the two Parties.

You see, you can't just sit down and cut out a Nation on the map. Look at President Wilson, who had the greatest ideas in the world, and meant the best in the world; but somebody gave him the map of Europe—they handed it to him in the nature of a Puzzle, to try and use all the blocks and put them together. Well, he took them and he got them all in the same amount of space they come out of, but they don't make a perfect Picture. Poland is composed of Czechs, Germans, Russians and Poles. He just took a little everywhere.

111

Then they said they wanted a Seacoast. They had never had one or seen one, but they wanted one. So they all got together to figure out how to let Poland see the ocean without trespassing. So they figured out that the only way was by a Corridor, or a kind of an alley, that they cut right through Germany. It would be like Oklahoma saying "I want to get to the ocean or Gulf," and you would split Texas half in two to let Oklahoma have a peep at the ocean. Only Germany can't get across from one part of their Country to another without having a passport to cross Poland.

Everybody that could think of a name they gave them a Country. It was a good idea; but it was kinder like giving every man his own Government. None of us relish being ruled by anybody else, but sometimes it is better. Now they all have to keep their own Armies and patrol their own borders and have their own Customs officers, and all the expense of their own Government and learning how to run it. You see, the more Nations you create, the more chances you have of war. You divide America into forty-seven different Nations, all with their own Laws, own Customs and own Management, and you would average, according to the best statistics available, about twenty-three wars a year. That's self-disintegration of small Nations.

And another thing that[284] is a big boost for more wars is the number of Countries that have a great amount of dissatisfied people in them. Well, every Nation has them; they are against the prevailing Government. Now they haven't got any Military Power and practically no strength at all, but they are just laying waiting till their Nation goes to a war with some outside Nations, and while it is engaged there they step in and cop off the Government. That's when all the Revolutions start—during a General war. You see, they can't attack their own Government in peacetime—they haven't got the power—but if they can get them shooting at somebody else, why, then they can go in and bring home the bacon.

You don't know how many people in every country are pulling for a revolution. The outs always think that that will give them a chance to get in. So you see, it is harder to overcome wars than you would at first think. Of course, this is not an argument to say that you shouldent try. For why they want to fight is more than I will ever know. Now this trouble over here about these debts, that goes further back than the debts.[285]

The main thing is a misunderstanding about the amount we did in the war. It is a favorite topic over here to belittle what we did in the war, and we think we helped them out quite a bit; and it is over that that the trouble is, and not over a few millions of Pounds or Francs. If we thought that they really at heart and conscientiously appreciated what we did in the war, I think there would be no trouble to get the debt canceled in full. But they at heart don't seem to think we did very much, so there the real trouble lies. There is just a misunderstanding about the real value of America's services in the war. It has been quite a good while since they were saved, and they are not willing to admit that they were saved. Just money never made friends with anybody. If a few millions of dollars is going to part our friendship, why, the friendship was never very deep. America feels they are not out buying people's friendship. If they can't do it by associating with them, and helping them in a common cause and going through a war with them, why, presenting them with a few million is not going to help us out.

You hear a lot about doing things to foster good relations between nations. The worst thing and the worst word that come out of the entire war was "propaganda." Propaganda means doing something for a reason; or, in other words, acting a part for a cause. Well, if we can't act natural and have people like us for what we really are, why, all the propaganda in the world will do no good. Propaganda is the easiest thing in the world detected, and the nation or individual that you are trying it on is the first to detect it.

There is nothing in the world that makes an individual so mad as to know that someone is trying to do some certain thing to curry favor with him, and it is the same with Nations.

Let a Nation do like an individual—that is, I mean a real individual. Let 'em go through life and do and act like they want to, and if they can't gain friends on their own accounts, don't let's go out and try and buy it. Any time you go out purposely to make friends with someone, the result is generally terrible. It's this trying to stand in that has got us where we are. If we would stay at home and quit trying to prowl around to various conferences and conventions somewhere, we would be better off.

We, unfortunately, don't make a good impression collectively. You see a bunch of Americans at anything abroad and they generally make more noise and have more to say than anybody, and generally create a worse impression than if they had stayed at home. They are throwing rocks at us, but sometimes you think it is deserved. There should be a law prohibiting over three Americans going anywhere abroad together.

But here is what I want you to get clear, Cal, when they talk about us being in so bad: Say, we haven't started to get in bad. Some of these Nations have been hating each other for generations, while they are only just starting in hating us. Some of them can't hate us so much, because we have never fought against them in their lives and have never taken any land away from them. So when it comes to being in wrong in Europe we are only an Amateur. It certainly don't take much diplomacy to tell what to do in International affairs from the experience we have had in the last few years—including Tacna Arica.[286] It didn't take us long to get in bad down there, as it did in Europe. All we have to do to get in bad is just to start out on what we think is a good-Samaritan mission, and we wind up in the Pesthouse.

All we have to do to get in bad is just to start out on what we think is a good Samaritan mission.

So, Cal, will you please do me and America a favor? If you see some Guy that looks like he is going off to some Convention or to attend something, will you kindly take a granite bowlder from the old Vermont hillside and just casually try and dent it on his bean? This applies everywhere. Will you please get all organizations and people belonging to them to stay at home and just for the novelty of the thing tend to our own business for a while? We take up with ideas so quick, I bet you it wouldent be any time before we would begin liking taking care of our own business. If somebody comes along with a war, why, don't even give him any publicity on it. With all the fool Conventions and Conferences we have over home, if a man can't get away from his wife enough attending them, then take his badges away from him.

114

If you see a Committee starting anywhere, deport them to Atlanta and let them join something there, And if Argentine, Brazil, Peru, Chile or anybody else have any disputed Territory and they want to populate it, or the Amazon, or the Andes, or Tacna Arica, or Tincture of Arnica, or anything else, with Peruvians, Chileans, Llamas, Boa Constrictors, Petrified Mummies or fertilizing Nitrates, why, let them go ahead and do it. What business is it of ours? If we have any Foreign Relations Committee, discharge them with our Foreign Relations and take the money we save by it and spend it on Better Babies Week.

It will take America fifteen years steady taking care of our own business and letting everybody else's alone to get us back to where everybody speaks to us again.

I could have prevented this whole debt argument, and all this hatred would never have come up. I WOULDENT HAVE LET THEM HAD THE MONEY IN THE FIRST PLACE!

But don't you let them work on your sympathy; and I don't believe they will be able to work on yours. These Birds are not doing as bad as they let on. If France ever paid their Taxes once, they would be the richest Nation in the world. And England has more money invested in Dress Suits and Dinner Jackets than America has in plows and farming utensils.

Now you just take this tip from your Apartment House in Europe. I am mighty glad you dident answer Clemenceau's open letter, because you hadent answered any of mine, and it would have made me look kinder bad to have had you answer his.[287]

I may drop over myself, as I have a lot of stuff that I will have to go over with you personally. I havent gone into it with you on this Russian thing since I come back from there. I think if you will take my tips I will be able to keep us out of war, and that will be more than any other Unofficial Diplomat has accomplished. Mellon is here just living off his interest. Senator Caraway, Pat Harrison, Barney Baruch and Jimmy Cox[288] are all here. Just think, four-fifths of the Democratic Party here at once. They are waiting for the other fifth— Upshaw, of Georgia. I am looking over Ireland and will report next week. London is pretty dull. The King is in Scotland shooting at a Grouse. Ambassador Houghton and Harry Lauder and some Scotchmen are helping to drive him up to the gun. The Duke of York is gone to Australia. Lady Astor has gone to America, and I have nowhere to eat now. Most everybody is out of London. There is practically nobody left but Dorothy Gish, Nora Bayes,[289] Mrs. Rogers and Myself, and Jim and Mary. Oh, yes, the Prince of Wales is visiting England now.[290]

If you see some Guy looks like he is going off to some convention or to attend something will you kindly take a granite boulder from the old Vermont hillside and dent it on his bean.

Poincaré will soon be retired for old age and long services rendered. He has been Prime Minister steady now for almost six weeks. Mellon says he did nothing here in Europe of a financial nature, but he deals in such big sums that a couple of billion loan to somebody wouldent be considered Finance by him.

Well, must stop.[291] Hope everything goes K. O. with you at the coming election. I think I will be over there to make that. About the only sure-fire money there is in Politics now is around election time. What state do you figure I could do better in? I bet you in about two more years Henry Ford will have enough to run for the Senate on.

Remember the next vacation is at Claremore. If you give us some money for a River and Harbor Bill, why, you can tie the old Barge Mayflower right down behind the pasture.

Yours Diplomatically at all times.

I certainly want you to know that this is a labor of love that I am doing for you, and I hope to be rewarded in '28.

Affectionately yours,

WILLIE.

P.S. Like all Ambassadors, I am underpaid and had to do something to raise some personal money. A man can't live abroad and entertain and eat both on the present Salaries, and so naturally I had to go to work.

It was embarrassing, but I had to do it; so I am at a Theater here. But please have it understood that the old remark about telling the Englishmen the joke one year and going back and hearing him laugh the next is all the bunk; he has a lot of Humor. Americans come over here and use slang and expect them to get it, and they dont; they could do the same with us. But they sure do know all the topical things, and read more than the people in big Cities at home, but no more than the ones in smaller towns or the Country. I never had a better audience, and they don't want you to compliment them; they have never had it, and they don't want it.

But it is humiliating to have to resort to menial labor in order to get back to report to you.

I want you to get Fletcher a House. Herrick and Houghton have got one. Maybe Mellon will do something for me, but I doubt it.

W. R.[292]

Special Cable

CALCOOL, *Whitewashhouse:*

LONDON, August 30.—Parliament met today. One member was thrown out. It seemed like Washington.[293]

Every foreigner is tickled over Newt Baker's[294] canceling of all debts.

Hobbs,[295] the English cricket champion, hits 316 runs and still is not out. Wake up, "Babe."

Daily Channel catastrophe: A German swam in here today from

Germany, got one look at England, turned around and is swimming back.[296]

Yours for the latest Channel news,

WILLROG.

Special Cable

CALCOOL, *Whitehousewash:*

LONDON, August 31.—Since a mother swam the Channel there has been no living with my wife over here. Will you please find out for me if this German who swam it is a father? If he was not I will give $500 to the first father that swims it and $1000 to the first grandfather.

Yours for equality in sex,

WILLROG.

Special Cable

CALCOOL, *Washhousewhite:*

LONDON, Sept. 1.—Former Secretary of State Hughes[297] had an interview with former Premier Briand of France, but nothing official transpired, as neither carried an employe's card.

Russia wants to discuss debt payments with us. If you promise to pay America, it will loan you twice as much as you promise to pay. Wise guys, those Russians. I see Newt is entered for the 1928 Democratic Follies.

Yours in exile,

WILLROG.

Special Cable

CALCOOL, *Whitewashhouse:*

LONDON, Sept. 3.—The League of Nations to perpetuate peace is in session. On account of Spain not being in the last war, they won't let her in. If you want to help make peace you have to fight for it.

Yours for peace without politics,

WILLROG.

Special Cable

CALCOOL, *Washhousewhite:*

LONDON, Sept. 5.—I see where you say if Europe doesn't disarm you will build another airship.[299] Just as well start it for nobody here is going to do any disarming.

118

The way to make them disarm is to start building and quit begging them to disarm.[300]

Yours for a nation of high fliers,

WILLROG.

Special Cable

CALCOOL, *Whitewashhouse:*

LONDON, Sept. 6.—I see by the Paris papers that Harry and Evelyn[301] are going back together again. Well, everybody wishes them lots of happiness.

That brings up a mighty good idea. Let everybody go back and start in with the original wives. In nine cases out of ten it will be found that they were the best after all.

Can you imagine the scramble in Hollywood trying to locate the original wife?

Yours for originality,

WILLROG.[302]

Special Cable

CALCOOL, *Washhousewhite:*

DUBLIN, Sept. 8.—It is so peaceful and quiet here in Dublin that it is almost disappointing.

Even the Irish themselves are beginning to get used to it and like it. They even have a representative at the Peace Conference.

Ireland treats you more like a friend than a tourist.

President Cosgrave sends regards to prospective President Smith.

Yours without blarney,

WILLROG.[303]

Special Cable

CALCOOL, *Whitehousewash:*

LONDON,[304] Sept. 12.—I saw a German outrun the great Finnish runner Nurmi yesterday and a Swede do it this afternoon.[305] If a different nationality is going to beat him every day, I'm taking him on Wednesday.

This has been great three days for Germany; they won a foot race and got into the League of Nations. They feel that these two events will just set them in right for the next war.

All the Channel swimming was called off today on account of rain and a wet track.

Yours for ein dunkle and ein heller,

WILLROG.

CALCOOL, *Whitehousewash:*

PARIS, Sept. 17.—I've been away up in the mountains of Switzerland and couldn't get any word to you for a few days. If you didn't yodle it they couldn't read it.

France said at the League the other day that her and Germany were old pals again. I guess they are; floated down the Rhine in Germany all day yesterday and there was so many French soldiers in the way I couldn't see the castles.[306]

WILLROG.

Special Cable

CALCOOL, *Whitewashhouse:*

PARIS, Sept. 20.—I've been reading about the primary elections over home. Looks like everybody that remains honest is getting beat.[308]

Yours,

WILLROG.

Special Cable

CALCOOL, *Washhousewhite:*

Aboard S. S. "Leviathan," Sept. 22.—On board the "Leviathan" with twenty-five hundred last surviving American tourists. Have all their friends meet them at boat with tip and taxi fare. Most of them have drank up their baggage already.

Yours for deep sea news,

WILLROG.

Special Cable

CALCOOL, *Washhousewhite:*

Aboard S. S. "Leviathan," Sept. 23.—Some Americans in Europe are traveling incognito. They are not bragging on where they come from, and nobody knows they are Americans.

Yours for maritime news,

WILLROG.[309]

Special Cable

CALCOOL, *Washhousewhite:*

On board the "Leviathan," Sept. 26.— Everybody on the boat is having a hard time packing, trying to make bottles look like soiled clothing.

Secretary Hughes and I are coming into New York with one of the best benefit acts in the show business.[310] I hate to see the team break up. Mr. Hershey[311] of Hershey, Pa. gave us $8,000 more this afternoon for Florida for repeating the act.

Hope my wife gets her Irish table linens in free. Back home and broke.

WILLROG.

NOTES

¹ Grace Goodhue Coolidge (1879-1957). Rogers once referred to the president's wife as "Public Female Favorite No. 1." She was a gracious and popular first lady—more personable than the president—and increased the number of entertainers invited to the White House, including Will Rogers who spent a night there following his trip abroad in 1926. (See footnote 6.)

² Nancy Langhorne Astor (1879-1964). Wife of Lord Waldorf Astor and first woman to sit in the House of Commons (1920-1944). Born in Virginia, Lady Astor was one of five girls known as the beautiful Langhorne sisters; extremely popular international figure.

³ Alice Roosevelt Longworth (1884-   ). Daughter of President Theodore Roosevelt, wife of Speaker of the House Nicholas Longworth, and famous Washington hostess. Alice Longworth, a close friend of Will Rogers, was known for her influence and colorful commentary on politics and current affairs. (See footnotes 15 and 38.)

⁴ H(erbert) G(eorge) Wells (1866-1946). Talented and controversial English novelist, historian and popularizer of new ideas; wrote *The Invisible Man* (1897), *The War of the Worlds* (1898), *Outline of History* (1920) and other works. By 1926 he had emerged as a popular celebrity with each new shift in his opinions announced through syndicated articles.

⁵ Theodore Dreiser (1871-1945). Novelist whose *Sister Carrie* (1900)) and *An American Tragedy* (1925) are classic examples of naturalism in American writing. Rogers here referred to *An American Tragedy,* a massive work comprising three book length parts in one volume, which told of a poor young man's futile effort to achieve social and financial success; the attempt ended in his execution for murder.

⁶ (John) Calvin Coolidge (1872-1933). Lieutenant governor of Massachusetts (1916-1918); governor (1919-1920); vice president of the United States (1921-1923). Succeeded to the presidency on the death of Warren Harding and served from 1923-1929. Coolidge, quiet and reserved, was known popularly as "Silent Cal." (See footnote 24.)

⁷ Nicholas Murray Butler (1862-1947). Professor of philosophy and education at Columbia University (1890-1901); president of Columbia (1902-1945) and other schools; president of Carnegie Endowment for International Peace (1925-1945). Author of books on educational and public problems.

⁸ Frank Waterman Stearns (1856-1939). Wealthy and progressive Boston merchant. Supported and promoted Calvin Coolidge's election as lieutenant governor and governor of Massachusetts and later as vice president. Coolidge's closest associate and confidant. At Harding's death, Coolidge gave a permanent suite in the White House to Stearns and his wife.

⁹ William Morgan Butler (1861-1939). U. S. senator (1924-1926); chairman of the Republican national committee (1924). Influential politician from Massachusetts. Adviser to President Coolidge and spokesman for the president while in the senate.

¹⁰ *Saturday Evening Post* (hereafter cited *SEP;* July 10, 1926, p. 3): . . . *But with an election coming on this fall he wouldent* . . .

¹¹ The United States government loaned more than $10 billion to several foreign nations during and immediately after World War I. The repayment of these loans was exceedingly difficult, for many of the indebted nations were beset with reconstruction costs, economic instability and scarcity of surplus monies. Moreover, some countries particularly France, believed that the loans should be considered America's equivalent of the blood and treasure expended by its allies in winning the war.

¹² *SEP* (July 10, 1926, p. 3): . . . *fool* . . .

¹³ Rogers might have referred here to Walter Lippman (1889-1974). American political journalist and author. Associate editor of the *New Republic* (1914-1917; 1919-1920); assistant to the secretary of war (1917); secretary of preparatory organization for Paris peace conference (1918-1919). Author of *A Preface to Politics* (1913), *Public Opinion* (1922) and other works.

14 Will Rogers was born November 4, 1879, near what is now Oologah, Oklahoma. Nearby Claremore, county seat of Rogers County, named for Will's father, Clement Vann Rogers, was the home of the elder Rogers for many years; Will Rogers mentioned frequently that it was his home, also. He explained that he claimed Claremore was his home because "only another Indian could pronounce Oologah." Many people have believed erroneously that Claremore was Rogers' birthplace.

15 Theodore Roosevelt (1858-1919). Republican governor of New York (1899-1900); vice president of the United States (1901); president of the United States (1901-1909). Roosevelt organized the first volunteer cavalry regiment during Spanish-American War (1898), and as its commander served in Cuba. The United States had blamed Spain for the sinking of the American warship *Maine* in a Cuban harbor; the loss of the *Maine* and its crew prompted in part the American declaration of war on Spain.

16 Charles Nathaniel Haskell (1860-1933). Democratic governor of Oklahoma (1907-1911).

17 Al Jennings (1863-1961). Attorney for Canadian County, Oklahoma (1892-1893); ran a distant third in Oklahoma's Democratic gubernatorial primary of 1914. Jennings was known mainly for having served a term in federal prison for robbery of the United States mails and assault on a federal officer. Later he produced and acted in western movies.

18 John Callaway "Jack" Walton (1881-1949). Mayor, Oklahoma City, Oklahoma (1919-1923); Democratic governor of Oklahoma (1923). Impeached and convicted of several charges including excessive and illegal spending in his primary campaign and padding the state payroll. Began his tenure as governor on January 9, 1923, with a gigantic barbecue on the state fair grounds.

19 William Jennings Bryan (1860-1925). Bryan was the Democratic candidate for president in 1896, 1900 and 1908. Served as Wilson's secretary of state (1913-1915). In the campaign of 1896, Bryan was supported by three parties and waged a vigorous campaign, traveling 13,000 miles in fourteen weeks, making 600 speeches in twenty-nine states.

20 William Howard Taft (1857-1930). Governor of the Philippine Islands (1901-1904); provisional governor of Cuba (1906); Republican president of the United States (1909-1913); chief justice of the Supreme Court (1921-1930). Weighed in excess of 300 pounds.

21 (Thomas) Woodrow Wilson (1856-1924). Democratic governor of New Jersey (1911-1913); president of the United States (1913-1921). In his presidential campaign of 1912, Wilson attracted many liberal western Democrats, most important of them Colonel Edward M. House of Texas (see footnote 30). House was drawn instantly and permanently to Wilson and proceeded to convert William J. Bryan and others to Wilson's support.

22 Thomas Riley Marshall (1854-1925). Democratic governor of Indiana (1909-1913); popular two-term vice president in Woodrow Wilson's administration (1913-1921).

23 Will H(arrison) Hays (1879-1954). American lawyer and politician; chairman, Republican national committee (1918-1921); United States postmaster general (1921-1922); president, Motion Picture Producers and Distributors of America (1922-1945). Hays was a public relations expert and manager-in-chief of Warren Harding's campaign of 1920.

24 Warren Gamaliel Harding (1865-1923). U. S. senator (1915-1921); received the Republican nomination for president on the tenth ballot in 1920. Popular misconception that his nomination was secured in a "smoke-filled room" by political cronies. Served three years as president (1921-1923) and died in office.

25 The Democratic national convention of 1924 was one of the most bitter and hard-fought gatherings in the party's history. The two principal candidates, Georgia prohibitionist William G. McAdoo (see footnote 182) and New York wet Alfred E. Smith (see footnote 41), battled each other through 102 ballots before the fractured nomination went to a West Virginia statesman, John W. Davis (see footnote 277), on the 103rd and final ballot.

26 *SEP* (July 10, 1926, p. 4): . . . *on through THE SATURDAY EVENING POST.*

27 The state reformatory at Elmira, New York, which was first opened in 1876, was a minimum-security prison for young adult first offenders. In the

fall of 1925 Rogers opened a personal tour of the country with a performance in Elmira.

²⁸ Jack Dempsey (1895-). World's heavyweight boxing champion (1919-1926).

Peggy Hopkins Joyce (1893-1957). Ziegfeld *Follies* beauty whose six marriages brought her much publicity.

Edward Albert Christian George Andrew Patrick David (1894-1972). Prince of Wales, became King of England as Edward VIII in January 1936. He was king only eleven months, for on December 11, 1936, he abdicated the throne to marry an American divorcee, Mrs. Wallis Warfield Simpson. The former king was given the title Duke of Windsor. He was an avid sportsman and had played polo with Will Rogers.

James Edward "Pa" Ferguson (1871-1944). Democratic governor of Texas (1915-1917); impeached for several reasons including misappropriation of state funds. He attempted to run again in 1924, but a court ruled he could not be a candidate. His wife, Miriam Wallace Ferguson (1875-1961), promptly entered the race and won with the open support of her husband. "Ma" Ferguson served from 1925-1927 and 1933-1935.

David Lloyd George (1863-1945). British statesman. Chancellor of the exchequer (1908-1915); secretary of state for war (1916). Replaced Earl of Asquith as prime minister (1916-1922) and directed Britain's policies to victory in World War I and in settlement of terms of peace.

Coleman Livingston Blease (1868-1942). Democratic governor of South Carolina (1911-1915): U. S. senator (1925-1931).

Paul von Hindenburg (1847-1934). German military officer and state official. Hindenburg had retired (1911) as an army corps commander but returned to military duty at the outbreak of World War I, eventually serving as army chief of staff (1916-1919). Following his second retirement (1919), Hindenburg was elected second president (1925-1932) of the German Weimar Republic and reelected (1932-1934), defeating Adolf Hitler at the polls. Compelled to yield to Nazi power by appointing Hitler chancellor (1933).

Thomas Lindsay Blanton (1872-1957). Democratic U. S. representative from Texas (1917-1929: 1930-1937).

Benito Mussolini (1883-1945). Italian dictator (1922-1943) and founder of the fascist movement in Italy. Reformed government and made domestic improvements which initially impressed Will Rogers and others.

Aimee Semple McPherson (1890-1944). American evangelist in the 1920s who was founder of the International Church of the Foursquare Gospel.

²⁹ Charles Gates Dawes (1865-1951). American lawyer, financier and politician. Vice president of the United States in Coolidge's administration (1925-1929). Originated the Dawes plan for solving the German reparation payment question. Dawes wrote letters to leading Europeans announcing Rogers' tour of Europe.

³⁰ Edward Mandell House (1858-1938). Served as President Wilson's adviser and closest associate during his administration.

³¹ Friedrich Wilhelm Viktor Albert (1859-1941). Kaiser Wilhelm II, emperor of Germany and king of Prussia (1888-1918). Sided with Austria-Hungary in crisis with Serbia (1914); dominant force of Central Powers at beginning of World War I. Saw influence and power decline; abdicated (November 28, 1919) and fled to Holland.

³² On October 16, 1901, Dr. Booker T. Washington, noted black American scientist and educator, dined at the White House at the invitation of President Theodore Roosevelt. The incident raised considerable controversy for it marked the first time a black person officially had been invited to dine at the White House.

³³ On February 16, 1926, Rogers had dinner—went out for chili—with Texas Governor Miriam "Ma" Ferguson and her husband, James "Pa" Ferguson, when Rogers was in Austin, Texas, for a speaking engagement.

³⁴ Dawes European Campaign. Dawes campaigned extensively abroad and in the United States for his plan for payment of German reparations.

³⁵ Rogers referred to an embarrassing incident for Dawes six days after his inauguration. Vice President Dawes, presiding officer of the senate, had gone to the Willard Hotel near the capitol for a nap while members of the senate debated confirmation of an appointee of Coolidge. A vote was called,

resulting in a tie; but Dawes returned too late. A Democrat changed his vote and Coolidge's appointment was denied. Dawes' influence in the Republican party rapidly diminished thereafter.

[36] James Alexander Reed (1861-1944). Democratic U. S. senator from Missouri (1911-1929). Acrimonious foe of Dawes.

[37] William Edgar Borah (1865-1940). Republican U. S. senator from Idaho (1907-1940). In the 1920s Borah was powerful force in foreign affairs; he initiated the Washington conference of 1921 and was chairman of the senate committee on foreign relations from 1924. He was a widely known isolationist, for he had opposed vehemently the League of Nations.

[38] Nicholas Longworth (1869-1931). Ohio state representative (1899-1900); state senator (1901-1903); Republican U. S. representative (1903-1913; 1915-1931); speaker of the house of representatives (1925-1931); husband of Alice Roosevelt Longworth.

James Wolcott Wadsworth, Jr. (1877-1952). New York state legislator (1905-1910); Republican U. S. senator (1915-1927); U. S. representative (1933-1951).

Alice Hay Wadsworth. Socialite and wife of Senator James W. Wadsworth, Jr., of New York; daughter of John Milton Hay, secretary of state (1898-1905) in the administrations of William McKinley and Theodore Roosevelt.

[39] James Thomas Begg (1877-1963). Republican U. S. representative from Ohio (1919-1929).

[40] John Nance Garner (1868-1967). Texas state representative (1898-1902); Democratic U. S. representative (1903-1933); minority floor leader (1929-1931); speaker of the house (1931-1933); vice president of the United States (1933-1941).

Finis James Garrett (1875-1956). Democratic U. S. representative from Tennessee (1905-1929); minority floor leader (1923-1929).

[41] Alfred Emanuel Smith (1873-1944). New York state legislator (1903-1915); governor (1919-1921; 1923-1929); sought the Democratic presidential nomination in 1920 and 1924 and finally became the nominee in 1928. His Catholicism and adamant opposition to prohibition dampened his political success.

[42] Henry Prather Fletcher (1873-1959). Career American diplomat; U. S. minister to Chile (1909); ambassador to Chile (1914), Mexico (1916-1920), Belgium (1922-1924) and Italy (1924-1929). Chairman of the Republican national committee (1934-1936). Four attempts on Mussolini's life occurred between November 1925 and October 1926. Each was followed by violent retaliation against anti-fascists, despite orders to the contrary from Mussolini.

[43] *SEP* (July 10, 1926, p. 54): . . . *next open-air* . . .

[44] *SEP* (July 10, 1926, p. 54): . . . *that I was fortunate in going to Italy, as this* . . .

[45] *SEP* (July 10, 1926, p. 54): . . . *ankle," meaning that he wore them, but that he dident mean that he wore them.*

[46] Sol Bloom (1870-1949). Democratic U. S. representative from New York (1923-1949). Previously engaged in the newspaper, theatrical and music-publishing businesses.

[47] Harold Edward "Red" Grange (1904-   ). Star football halfback for the University of Illinois (1922-1925); left college to sign with a professional football team, the Chicago Bears. Grange played with the Bears from 1925 to 1934 and later coached and broadcasted sports events.

[48] In 1917 American government officials seized the *Leviathan,* then known as the *Vaterland,* from its German owners as it sat in berth in Hoboken, New Jersey. The *Leviathan,* one of the premier luxury liners of the 1920s, was rechristened and eventually sold to the United States Lines. The ship was sold in 1937 to British interests after having been idle for three years.

[49] Andrew William Mellon (1855-1937). Conservative Republican financier; secretary of treasury (1921-1932) in three Republican administrations.

[50] Harry Stewart New (1858-1937). Indiana state senator (1896-1900); Republican U. S. senator (1917-1923); appointed postmaster general in Harding's cabinet on February 27, 1923; reappointed by Coolidge and served from 1923-1929.

[51] William Ashley "Billy" Sunday (1862-1935). Popular evangelist who reached the height of his career in the 1920s.

[52] According to Cherokee tribal rolls, Will Rogers was 9/32 Cherokee—or about a fourth.

[53] Samuel F. Kingston (1866?-1929). Irish-born Kingston managed several early-day theatrical stars including Billie Burke. He later served as manager and casting director for the Fox picture corporation. From 1919-1929 he was general manager for Florenz Ziegfeld's operations and second only to Ziegfeld in that large organization.

[54] Florenz Ziegfeld (1867-1932). American theatrical producer. Organized the popularly known Ziegfeld's *Follies* in which Rogers and others performed and starred.

[55] Rogers referred to the first of his three children: William Vann Rogers (1911-   ). His other children, Mary Amelia Rogers (1913-   ) and James Blake Rogers (1915-   ), and his wife, Betty Blake Rogers (1879-1944), joined Rogers and Will, Jr. in England a few months later. Will, Jr. returned to the United States early to enroll in Culver Military Academy in Indiana for the fall school term.

[56] Sandy Hook is a peninsula of New Jersey, located fifteen miles south of Manhattan Island. The Sandy Hook lighthouse, constructed in 1763, is the oldest lighthouse operating in the United States and a favorite orientation point for ship captains operating along the middle Atlantic coast.

[57] Frank Billings Kellogg (1856-1937). Republican U. S. senator from Minnesota (1917-1923); United States ambassador to Great Britain (1923-1925); secretary of state (1925-1929). With Aristide Briand, French prime minister, negotiated antiwar treaty (Kellogg-Briand pact), signed at Paris (1928). (See footnote 181.)

[58] Following World War I, several new nations were created in southern and eastern Europe due to the break-up of the Austro-Hungarian Empire and redrawing of other national boundaries. President Woodrow Wilson and other world leaders had campaigned strongly for this idea of national self-determination.

[59] Rogers referred to the depressed condition of American agriculture. While the business and industrial sectors enjoyed relative prosperity, huge surpluses of crops and stock, low market prices and other problems plagued the American farmer. After considerable debate Congress passsed the McNary-Haugen bill, designed to relieve farmers of their large surpluses. However, Coolidge considered the measure unconstitutional and cumbersome and eventually vetoed it. His opposition raised the ire of many farmers of both political parties.

[60] *SEP* (July 17. 1926, p. 6): Omitted: *White House, Washington, D. C.*
MR. CALVIN COOLIDGE:
Certain news is so urgent that it is necessary for me to cable you, so from time to time you may get something "Collect." I hope there is an appropriation to cover this, look under the heading "Ways and Means."
WILLROG *(diplomatic code name).*

[61] Herbert Hartley (1876-1957). Commander of the *Leviathan* (1923-1928). Became friend of rulers, business tycoons, adventurers and movie stars, including Will Rogers.

[62] *SEP* (July 17, 1926, p. 6): Omitted: . . . *—especially when it's rough—* . . .

[63] The Preliminary Disarmament Conference was established by the League of Nations in 1925; functioned for five years planning for the worldwide disarmament conference held in 1932.

[64] Hugh Simons Gibson (1883-1954). American diplomat who was the first United States minister to Poland (1919-1924); also served as ambassador to Switzerland (1924-1927), Belgium (1927-1933; 1937-1938) and Brazil (1933-1937).

[65] *SEP* (July 17, 1926, p. 7): . . . *Title in between an Ambassador and a Consul.*

[66] Dennis Edward Nolan (1872-1953). Major general; chief of the intelligence service of the American Expeditionary Army in World War I.
George Veazey Strong (1880-1946). Major in the United States army; member, judge advocate general's department attached to the war plans division; technical adviser to the American delegation in Geneva.

[67] Hilary Pollard Jones (1863-1938). Rear admiral, United State navy; chairman of the executive committee of the naval general board; former commander in chief of the Atlantic fleet (1922-1923).
Andrew Theodore Long (1866-1946). Rear admiral, United States navy;

formerly chief of staff of the Atlantic fleet; naval attaché at Rome. The United States was represented in Geneva by Gibson, Jones, Long, seven other naval officers, a legal adviser, a state department adviser, a four-man secretariat and an archivisit. The army officers were not official delegates.

68 Adolphus Andrews (1879-1948). Captain Andrews had been in command of the presidential yacht, the *Mayflower,* from 1922 until he was selected to accompany the American delegation to Geneva; was responsible for Coolidge's safety during the president's weekend excursions down the Potomac River on the *Mayflower.*

69 Allen Welsh Dulles (1893-1969). Dulles was chief of the Near East division of the state department; legal adviser to the American delegation in Geneva; later director of the Central Intelligence Agency (1953-1961).

Dorsey Richardson (1896-1974). Assistant chief of the division of Western European affairs in the United States department of state; technical adviser to the conference until July 1926.

70 Rogers referred to the fact that as governor of Massachusetts, Coolidge ordered out the state militia to halt a police strike in Boston (1919). His firm action attracted the national acclaim which contributed to his selection as Warren G. Harding's running mate in 1920.

71 Woodrow Wilson was the first president to travel abroad while in office. He made two trips to Europe after World War I to further the post-war peace negotiations.

72 Fannie Ward (1875-1952). Although Fannie Ward, the actress, was fifty years old when Will Rogers wrote this book, Rogers mentions her in other writings as still beautiful and full of pep. Miss Ward performed in both the United States and England. Was famous for looking perpetually young.

73 Jackie Coogan (1914-   ). Child actor; would have been twelve years old when Will Rogers wrote this book. Starred with Charlie Chaplin in *The Kid* (1920).

74 Marcus Loew (1870-1927). American theater owner and motion picture producer. Co-founder and controller of Metro-Goldwyn-Mayer Corporation.

Lee Shubert (1875-1953). With his brother, Jacob J. (1880-1963), owned and managed numerous theaters inside and outside New York. Also produced several plays and shows. Introduced such stars as Al Jolson, Eddie Cantor, Ed Wynn, Fanny Brice, Ray Bolger, Bert Lahr and many others.

75 An "Annie Oakley" was a punched complimentary ticket derived from the famous markswoman Annie Oakley's trick shooting where she would riddle a playing card before it hit the ground.

76 The general council of the trades union congress of England called for a general strike of industrial and service workers to force the British government to subsidize the workers' low wages, particularly in coal mining. The strike began on May 3, 1926, but soon collapsed due to successful governmental efforts to continue services and industrial operations. The strike was called off on May 12, 1926.

77 The Eighteenth Amendment was ratified in 1919 and established prohibition of intoxicating liquors as a national policy. The Volstead Act (1919) provided the machinery for enforcement. It defined as intoxicating liquor any beverage containing more than one-half of one percent alcohol.

78 Edward Peter "Garet" Garrett (1878-1954). American journalist and economist who wrote popular books and articles on economic subjects.

79 Isaac Frederick Marcosson (1877-1961). American journalist and author; wrote for the *Saturday Evening Post* (1907-1910; 1913-1936). Author of *The Business of War* (1917) and *Peace and Business* (1919).

80 *SEP* (July 17, 1926, p. 157): . . . *had not interviewed, . . .*

81 Rogers planned to visit Russia, but he did not learn until later that his application to enter the country had been approved. His impressions of Russia were serialized originally in the *Saturday Evening Post* of October 23, November 6 and December 4, 1926, and published in book form by Albert & Charles Boni, Inc. in 1927, entitled *There's Not a Bathing Suit in Russia and Other Bare Facts.* It was reissued as Volume II, of Series I, of the Writings of Will Rogers (1973).

82 Gloria Swanson (Josephine May Swenson) (1899-   ). Glamorous American film, stage and television actress. She appeared in nearly fifty movies from 1913-1956.

83 *SEP* (July 17, 1926, p. 157): . . . *These are just little suggestions that might not be amiss to you every morning when the Farm relief Associations wakes you up.*

84 Henry Ford (1863-1947). Founder of Ford Motor Company and a close friend of Will Rogers.

85 James D. Preston (1876-1959). Cub reporter for the *Boston Journal;* supervisor of the senate press gallery (1897-1932).

86 *SEP* (July 17, 1926, p. 158): . . . *prayed. He seemed to be pretty well posted just on about what the needs and wants of the British Empire were. He* . . .

87 The Ku Klux Klan of the post-Civil War period was revived in 1915 and gathered thousands of converts during the 1920s through the promotional efforts of Edward Clarke and Elizabeth Tyler. The extremely nationalistic and racist Klan, 5,000,000 strong, was a major issue in the nation, flourishing in the North as well as in the South. In the election of 1924 Coolidge had avoided the Klan issue.

88 Randall Thomas Davidson (1848-1930). Archbishop of Canterbury, Church of England (1903-1928).

89 The Populist party flourished during the 1880s and 1890s as an agrarian protest against falling prices, poor credit and marketing facilities, and crop failures. Its fusion with the Democratic party in support of the latter's presidential candidate, William Jennings Bryan, and the subsequent defeat of Bryan in 1896 marked the end of the effectiveness of the Populists.

90 William David Upshaw (1866-1952). Democratic U. S. representative from Georgia (1919-1927); founder, *The Golden Age,* a magazine of militant Christian citizenship (1906).

91 *SEP* (July 17, 1926, p: 158): . . . *afternoon. And, say, wait a minute! He* . . .

92 Albert Frederick Arthur George (1895-1952). Duke of York; brother of Prince of Wales. Succeeded to English throne on May 12, 1937, after his brother abdicated. Became George VI.

93 *SEP* (July 17, 1926, p. 161): . . . *called Americano del Norte. Then* . . .

94 *SEP* (July 17, 1926, p. 161): . . . *the Follies will* . . .

95 Winston Leonard Spencer Churchill (1874-1965). Home secretary (1910-1911); chancellor of the exchequer of England (1924-1929); prime minister of England during World War II and early 1950s, serving from 1940-1945 and 1951-1955. Due to the shutdown of regular newpapers by striking printers, Prime Minister Stanley Baldwin directed Churchill to issue a daily paper. Churchill's one-sheet journal, the *British Gazette,* quickly became a propaganda tool of the government. (See footnote 124.)

96 Irene Langhorne Gibson (Mrs. Charles Dana Gibson) (1873-1956). Sister of Lady Nancy Astor and wife of Charles Dana Gibson (1867-1944), American illustrator who created the "Gibson Girl." Charles Gibson's work appeared in many of the major publications including *Scribner's, Harper's* and *Collier's Weekly.*

97 Carter Glass 1858-1946). Virginia state senator (1899-1902); Democratic U. S. representative (1902-1918); secretary of the treasury under Wilson (1918-1920); U. S. senator (1920-1946).

98 *SEP* (July 17, 1926, p. 161): . . . *wheezes. So later on I want to tell you what all happened in the next few days.*

The Prince phoned me—that is, his Equery, Gen. Trotter, did—and asked me over to his place, York House, and I want to tell you about all he asked about over home. He wanted to know how you were, Mr. President, and I want to tell you also how these English people . . .

99 James Gleason and Richard Taber wrote *Is Zat So?,* an amusing three-act play which billed itself as "The Comedy." It opened off-Broadway on January 5, 1925, and ran for 618 performances; opened in London at the Apollo Theatre on February 15, 1926, with Gleason and Robert Armstrong in the leading roles. (See footnote 136).

No! No! Nanette opened at the Palace Theatre in London in the spring of 1925 for an extended run of more than a year. Herbert Clayton and Jack Waller produced the two-act comedy which starred George Grossmith and Joseph Coyne. (See footnotes 134 and 135.)

Mercenary Mary opened on October 7, 1925, at the London Hippodrome and starred Sonnie Hale, A. W. Bascomb, Peggy O'Neil and Lew Hearn. Herbert Clayton and Jack Waller produced the two-act American musical comedy, and William B. Friedlander and Con Conrad co-authored the music.

Kid Boots first appeared in London on February 2, 1926, at the Winter Garden Theatre. Florenz Ziegfeld produced the two-act American musical comedy, and Harry Tierney wrote the score and lyrics. *Kid Boots* starred Leslie Henson in the London production and Eddie Cantor in the American production.

The Student Prince, the musical comedy version of *Old Heidelberg,* opened in London on February 3, 1926, at His Majesty's Theatre. Lee and J. J. Shubert, famed American theater owners and managers, staged the American play which was the first English production for the famous brothers. Sigmund Rombourg provided the music for *The Student Prince* which starred Allan Prior.

Lady Be Good opened at the Empire Theatre in London on April 13, 1926, following a successful run on Broadway. The popular brother and sister team of Fred and Adele Astaire starred in the George and Ira Gershwin musical and received one of the warmest welcomes ever accorded an American actor or actress in London.

100   *Abie's Irish Rose* enjoyed one of the longest runs in the history of New York theater productions. Anne Nichols wrote the comedy which opened May 23, 1922, and played before approximately 2,000,000 viewers during 2,357 performances on Broadway.

101   Paul Whiteman (1891-1967). American bandleader who became famous in the 1920s for pioneering "sweet style" as opposed to the traditional "classical" style of jazz.

102   Fritz Kreisler (1875-1962). American violinist who composed arrangements of classical music for violins and the operetta *Apple Blossoms* (1919).

103   Ignace Jan Paderewski (1860-1941). Polish composer, pianist and patriot who as pianist/composer worked to aid Polish relief during World War I. In January 1919 became prime minister and minister of foreign affairs of Poland; resigned in November 1919 because he was unable to unify the country. Retired to California and returned to concert touring.

104   Alanson Bigelow Houghton (1863-1941). Republican U. S. representative from New York (1919-1922); ambassador to Germany (1922-1925); appointed as ambassador to Great Britain by President Coolidge; served from 1925-1929.

105   *SEP* (July 17, 1926, p. 162): . . . *the time comes.*

Well as I said before, I must have some pleasure along with all my business and confinement. I will go . . .

106   *SEP* (July 24, 1926, p. 10): . . . *always The British.*

By the way, that reminds me, I heard a fellow during the heated debate in the House of Commons get up and just say, "England will do her duty." And about two-thirds of them pounced on him and hollered, "What about London?" "What about Glaskie?" I think he meant Glasgow. So he had to take his words back and take in more territory. So in any of our conversations back and forth you and I must always speak of it as the British.

I dident see anybody in England excited or doing anything, so I am just getting that way myself. Then not hearing from you dident speed things up any. I just thought, well, if after me stopping the strike the least I was expecting was a note of just a little congratulation. But the Postman may bring one with the next Post—they call it Post, not mail. And I will be there to get it if it comes, because I wouldent miss the Postman's visit, for they wear the funniest Hats and Caps. It's like the old-time soldiers used to wear in one of our wars with them. In fact I think it's the same hats, as that was all they got out of that particular encounter. Well, they look funny nowadays, and I always stay up just to get a laugh out of his hat.

Of course it's all over now and is not a lot of news to you to read about the strike. But of course I will have to tell you about it, because it may be of some use to you in case something comes up over home. A Man in your position has to be just like a Soldier, and study the different wars, especially the winning ones, and he is supposed to profit by their experience. So of course what I am over here for is to observe and report.

The only trouble with you about handling a situation is that you do it so different from what it has ever been handled before that History don't do you much good. You and Mussolini have broken every law of precedent, and still you get away with it. So I doubt if my little detailed report will be of much use to you after all. Mind you, in all this whole business where the country and the people acted so calmly, people lose sight of the fact that England wasent dealing with strikers; they were just dealing with what looked to me like a bunch of men that quit work to go out and assist the government to get someone to take their place.

It was carried . . .

107 *SEP (July 24, 1926, p. 10): . . . know anything sir."*

So you see, Mr. President, that is why I think that I should tell you about it. It was a very unusual strike from many angles. They sent armored Cars out on the roads, and the Strikers, who had used these same Tanks and Cars during the war would explain to the young Soldiers just how to use them in case another war ever come up, and they got along wonderfully. It was really excellent training for the younger men to have the advice of these experts.

108 *SEP (July 24, 1926, p. 10): . . . just as scheduled.*

The Pallbearers says, "It may take us a little longer to reach the Cemetary than is usual, but we will eventually get him there. We don't know on what day or what month, but it's all the same; he must be buried in the end."

109 *SEP (July 24, 1926, p. 10): . . . stand so much.*

I just thought here is seven million people in this one town, and there is five million on what they call a strike in the entire England; And there hasent been a shot fired, a fight, an argument, or even a Bootlegger arrested. I thought I wish I was able to pay all of you peoples' fares over to Herrin, Illinois, on one of their Days De Fiesta and let you see something that in the true definition of the word is a strike.

Now I played West Frankfort, right near Herrin, and was over there and met a lot of their people, and they are as fine and law-abiding as any you will find anywhere over home. But I will give them credit. When they start out to do anything they put it on right. If it's a Strike, they show you a strike. Now I am not criticizing England for not anything exciting. But don't call a thing a strike unless it is a strike. That, of course, is the one thing where our temperments will never agree. They think a substitute is just as good. But if you . . .

110 *SEP (July 24, 1926, p. 11): . . . Strike or not.*

But they done mighty nobly. Both sides distinguished themselves as True Britons. I want to tell you confidentially, Mr. President, that being in the House of Commons, as I was every day, and hearing everything that went on, I was always listening in your favor. I want to tell you that the whole thing was due practically to one man and that was Premier Baldwin. There is a fellow that might be of use to us over there some time. He just turned out to be the ablest man that they have over here.

You see, he is an Ex-Workingman himself, and he carried the confidence of both sides. The Strikers felt that he would give them a square deal and so did the Government, and I heard him come into that Commons and talk to them when the thing was at its height, and they give him every attention both sides. And the funny part of it was that he seemed to please both sides.

Then I heard him when he come in there and announced that they had come to a settlement. He was as calm; no Conquering hero stuff. He dident come in as the Victor, although he had really done it; he was very modest and quiet. You know, you told me too look out for someone over here kinder on the quiet. Well, this Baldwin looks like about the best bet they have in England. I think we can get him later on, because for doing this work so well for them they will perhaps make him a Lord, and that will make him practically useless for any service over here. So if we can get him before that Calamity befalls him, he would be mighty cheap for us. I don't think he gets a lot where he is.

You see, the beauty about him over home would be that he could replace about the biggest part of the Senate. You see, that is eventually what we will have to come to in America some day in Governmental affairs. It will be ability instead of numbers. The law won't just say elect so many men each time. It will say hunt till you find a few good men and let the others go.

Don't let the law state how many men are to rule our Country. Leave the number optional, but bear down on the amount of ability. You see, sometimes you can find some man that knows just as much as a hundred other put to-geather. Well, take him and get rid of the hundred. It will take us time to get this into effect over there, I know. But I also know from what talks I have

131

*had with you that to let several go around there would be in accord with your
desires. We can always do those little things under the heading of Economy.
But the real reason will be to get 'em out of there.*

*Now I think that about covers the field along the Strike and economic lines.
As far as America learning anything from England's great strike, they haven't
learned anything, because England hasent had a strike yet.*

111   Albert Russel Erskine (1871-1933). A former bookkeeper who rose to
the vice-presidency of the Underwood Typewriter Company, and from 1915
until his death by suicide served as president of Studebaker Motor Company.

John North Willys (1873-1935). Began in bicycle business and then bought
Overland Automobile Company to manufacture Willys-Overland and other ve-
hicles (1907); U. S. ambassador to Poland (1930-1932).

112   Charles Michael Schwab (1862-1939). President of Carnegie Steel
Company (1897-1901); first president of United States Steel Company (1901-
1903); president and chairman of the board of Bethlehem Steel Corporation
(1904-1939).

113   This and succeeding *Special Cables* did not appear in the *SEP*. However, beginning on July 29, 1926, Rogers cabled the messages to the *New York
Times* (hereafter cited as *NYT*) which featured them in a box set apart from
the rest of the news. Rogers continued to send the *Times* "daily telegrams" which
later were syndicated and then appeared in the Boni edition of *Letters of a
Self-Made Diplomat to His President* as *Special Cables*. This *Special Cable*
regarding President Coolidge's rural opposition was datelined August 5, 1926,
and thus not the first "daily telegram" Rogers cabled. Several of the *Special
Cables* in the Boni edition do not occur in the same chronological sequence as
they first appeared in the *New York Times*.

114   *SEP:* Omitted letter of May 17, 1926.

115   Walter C. Hagen (1892-1969). Brilliant American professional golfer
of the 1920s and 1930s. Hagen, first of the showman golfers, won four British
open championships, two United States open championships, five United States
professional golfers association championships and other titles and tournaments.

116   Robert Tyre "Bobby" Jones (1902-1971). American amateur golfer,
possibly the game's greatest player. In an eight year career he entered twenty-
seven tournaments and won eighteen of them, including four United States open
crowns, five United States amateur championships and three British open titles.

117   *NYT* (August 20, 1926, p. 19): *LONDON, Aug. 19.*

118   *SEP* (July 24, 1926, p. 126): . . . *memory. So get busy Americans to
be envious of me.*

119   James Matthew Barrie (1860-1937). Scottish novelist and playwright
who is most famous for his book *Peter Pan* (1904) and the play *Little Minister*
(1891).

120   Between 1925-1926 Rogers wrote a series of twenty-six highly amusing
and successful advertisements for the American Tobacco Company under the
title of "Bull's Eye." Rogers permitted the use of his signature and picture in
the ads and freely admitted that he did not smoke.

121   Maude Adams (Maude Kiskadden) (1872-1953). American actress
who worked in Charles Frohman's stock company; starred in plays by Barrie as
Lady Babble in *Little Minister* and as the title character in *Peter Pan*. (See
footnote 122.)

122   Charles Frohman (1860-1915). American theatrical manager and producer who built up the Empire Stock Company and produced plays by leading
dramatists of the day including Sir James Barrie.

123   *SEP* (July 24, 1926, p. 126): . . . *years. It's a whole letter, Mr. President, in itself, and as the Boat sails Wednesday, I want this to reach you.
Then I think it's* . . .

124   Stanley Baldwin (1867-1947). Conservative prime minister of Britain
(1923-1924; 1924-1929; 1935-1937); served as chancellor of exchequer (1922-
1923) and arranged funding of the British debt to the United States.

125   This *Special Cable* regarding Lady Astor was the first of the "daily
telegrams." Rogers cabled the message to the editors of the *New York Times* on
July 29, 1926, and they published it the following day.

126   *NYT* (July 30, 1926, p. 19): . . . *ask my friend, Jimmy Walker, to
have New York take good care of her.* . . .

127   Gifford Pinchot (1865-1946). Political leader and conservationist who

was America's first professional forester as chief of the United States forest service, department of agriculture; professor of forestry at Yale University (1903-1936); Republican governor of Pennsylvania (1923-1927; 1931-1935).

George Wharton Pepper (1867-1961). Republican U. S. senator from Pennsylvania (1922-1927) and ardent supporter of President Coolidge.

128 William Scott Vare (1867-1934). U. S. representative (1912-1923; 1923-1927). Established a Republican political machine in Philadelphia that dominated the city by 1917; in the primary elections of 1926 he was a successful candidate for the Republican nomination to the United States senate, but the senate rejected his election due to excessive expenditures; served as senator from 1927 until his unseating on December 6, 1929.

129 Wilson McCargo "Pick" Cross (1871-1947). Cross went to England in 1905 representing the Pennsylvania Lubricating Company. Later, he headed the London-based firm of Vacuum Oil Company, Limited, which eventually was absorbed by Standard Oil Company of New York. Cross, a flamboyant character, was a founding member and eventual president of the Amercian Club, an organization of Americans in London, which was formed in July 1919.

130 *SEP* (July 24, 1926, p. 129): . . . *with a Vacuum Cleaner.*

131 Lord Ashfield (Albert Stanley) (1874-1948). Transportation expert who was born in England but emigrated to the United States at an early age with his family. London Subway Company hired Stanley to reorganize operation (1907); president of British board of trade (1916-1919); chairman, London passenger transport board (1933).

132 Thomas Robert Dewar (1864-1930). British sportsman and distiller who operated and expanded family distillery business, John Dewar & Sons; named baron (1919).

133 *SEP* (July 24, 1926, p. 129): . . . *Whisky, and he was at one time Lord Mayor of London.*

134 George Grossmith (1874-1935). English comedian and singer in light opera and musical comedies; reputed to have introduced the revue in England.

135 Joseph Coyne (1867-1941). American musical comedy star who appeared in many productions in the United States and England. His last recorded appearance on stage was in 1931. In 1926 Coyne and Grossmith co-starred in *No! No! Nanette* at the Palace Theatre in London.

136 James Gleason (1886-1959). American actor, director, producer, screenwriter and playwright. In 1926 he played the part of Hap Hurley in his own production of *Is Zat So?* at the Apollo Theatre in London.

137 Tom Webster (1890-   ?). English cartoonist; in 1919 became the political cartoonist for the London *Daily Mail;* his cartoons, published annually in book form, were widely popular.

138 Jay Norwood "Ding" Darling (1876-1962). American political cartoonist who illustrated for several newspapers but primarily for the Des Moines *Register* (from 1906); won two Pulitzer prizes for cartooning (1924, 1943).

William "Billy" (Addison) Ireland (1880-1935). American cartoonist who was on the staff of the *Evening Dispatch,* Columbus, Ohio (1899-1935.)

139 Lester Allen (1891-1949). English-born comedian, actor and veteran of minstrel shows; began his professional career as an acrobat with Barnum & Bailey's Circus. In the 1920s he was featured in many musicals such a Ziegfeld's *Follies,* George White's *Scandals* and *Les Maires Affairs.*

140 George White (1890-1968). American producer, director, lyricist and actor. Started his career as a dancer in vaudeville but is probably most famous for series of George White's *Scandals,* revues in which he produced, directed and acted.

141 *SEP* (July 24, 1926, p. 129): . . . *night of it.*
They had asked the Prince of Wales to come, but owing to the strike and all its difficulties he was not going out much. I felt kinder bad the Prince wasent there. But my goodness, look who we did have!

142 Harry Gordon Selfridge (1857-1947). American who moved to London (1906), and organized Selfridge & Company, which developed into one of the largest department stores in Europe.

143 Frank Winfield Woolworth (1852-1919). American merchant who opened his first five-cent store in 1879 and expanded until Woolworth's five-and-ten-cent stores became famous in many cities of the United States and Britain.

[144]   *SEP* (July 24, 1926, p. 129):
P. S. Everybody over here knows Borah. I don't know whether that is an asset or a liability to him. They have never heard of our Senate, but they know Borah.
[145]   "Yes, We Have No Bananas." Words and music by Frank Silver and Irving Cohn (1923); one of the most successful nonsense songs of the 1920s.
"Valencia." A popular song originally with French lyrics by Jose Padilla. Clifford Grey penned the English lyrics (1926). The song was introduced into the United States in a revue, *The Great Temptations* (1926).
[146]   Mistinguett (Jeanne Bourgeois) (1874-1956). French music hall star who was known chiefly for having "million-dollar legs," insured for $3-5 million. Made three trips to the United States, including 1926 when she went as a tourist.
[147]   *SEP:* Omitted first letter dated May 20, 1926.
[148]   Rogers referred to Vare's contested senatorial victory in Pennsylvania. Senate investigators discovered that Vare actually spent less in the primary election than his opponent Pepper, but the senate unseated the Philadelphian. At the same time, the senate investigated the election of Frank Leslie Smith (1867-1950) of Illinois and denied Smith his seat in the senate due to excessive expenditures, and because as chairman of the Illinois commerce commission Smith had received $158,000 for his campaign from Samuel Insull, Chicago utilities magnate.
[149]   Nick Altrock (1876-1965). Baseball pitcher and coach of early 1900s who became clown-coach with Washington Senators (1909-1933). Altrock teamed with fellow ballplayer Al Schacht to perform clown routine at every World Series from 1921 to 1933.
[150]   Albert Einstein (1879-1955). German-born theoretical physicist who emigrated to the United States in 1933. Einstein enunciated and published an account of his special theory of relativity (1905) and of his general theory (1916).
[151]   Joseph Gurney "Uncle Joe" Cannon (1836-1926). Republican U. S. representative from Illinois (1873-1891; 1893-1913) and speaker of the house of representatives (1903-1911). As speaker Cannon was accused of autocratic methods in controlling house procedure. His power was curtailed in March 1910 by a combination of both parties.
Chauncey Mitchell Depew (1834-1928). Wealthy railroad executive and Republican U. S. senator from New York (1899-1911). Depew was known as after-dinner speaker and wit whom Will Rogers admired and helped celebrate his ninetieth birthday.
[152]   Gerald Frederic Trotter (1871-1945). Trotter held the rank of colonel and honorary rank of brigadier general; gentleman usher to King George V (1919-1936) and groom-in-waiting to the Prince of Wales (1921-1936).
[153]   *SEP* (July 24, 1926, p. 129): . . . *Prince of Wales."*
I thought, well, I better talk to him. He is an awful nice fellow. He was over in America with the Prince and everybody liked him, and he only had one arm. So I says, "What do you want?"
[154]   *SEP* (July 24, 1926, p. 129): . . . *Come on over."*
Well, though the strike had ended, all the Taxicabs hadent gone back to work yet. But I found me one and I said, "Boy, drive me to York House and I will pay all fines." Well, he looked at me and then he thought of York House, and said to himself, "The Prince has an American Chef coming or a low menial of some description."
Say, listen I . . .
[155]   *SEP* (July 24, 1926, p. 129): . . . *one old Limy . . .*
[156]   The Prince of Wales had suffered numerous, highly publicized accidents during his riding career. In January 1926 he suffered a collarbone fracture after falling twice in two days.
[157]   *SEP* (July 24, 1926, p. 129): . . . *cool; that had it happened in America everybody would have thought they were having a Retake on the last war.*
[158]   *SEP* (July 24, 1926, p. 129): . . . *crazy. He is right up to now on everything. I just switched around to find out.*
[159]   George Lane (1856-1925). Lane owned a ranch in Alberta, Canada and was a friend of the Prince of Wales. He had purchased a ranch for the prince which adjoined Lane's Bar U ranch.

134

160   Guy Weadick (1885-1953). Weadick originated the Calgary Stampede in 1912 and later managed it (1923-1932). He owned and managed a combination dude-cattle ranch near High River, Alberta (1923-1950).

161   *SEP* (July 24, 1926, p. 130): . . . *folks that died . . .*

162   The Prince of Wales had two brothers: George, Duke of York (see footnote 91), and Henry, Duke of Gloucester (1900-1974). The British public and press named the royal trio "The Three Musketeers" because of their close companionship.

Victoria Alexandra Alice Mary (1897-1965). Princess Mary of England. In 1922 Princess Mary married Henry George Charles Lascelles, sixth earl of Harewood (1882-1947).

163   Rogers might have referred to (Giles) Lytton Strachey's highly acclaimed and widely read *Queen Victoria* (New York: Harcourt, Brace & Company, 1921). Strachey's biography of the nineteenth century English monarch was a best seller in 1922 and still popular in 1926.

164   Will Rogers was an avid and excellent polo player. In the period 1919 to 1939 the United States was the predominant polo nation, with a strong challenge from Argentina, due to the exploits of Lewis Lacey, David and John Miles and Jack Nelson. Lacey was an exceptional player who participated for Argentina and England. He often teamed with T. P. Melvill and other English riders in international tournaments.

165   *SEP* (July 24, 1926, p. 130): . . . *Baltimore.*
He even told me who's horse fell with him. It was yours, Mrs. Pad Rumsey's, that's who's it was.
I asked him . . .

166   *SEP* (July 24, 1926, p. 130): . . . *him. I told him neither had I.*

167   *SEP* (July 24, 1926, p. 130): . . . *him you havent said the half of it, Prince.*

168   *SEP* (July 24, 1926, p. 130): . . . *South America. Was surprised when I told him I had been there, because from the looks of me I hadent been anywhere outside of Rogers County, Oklahoma.*

169   *SEP* (July 24, 1926, p. 130): . . . *Africa. He said he was sorry he couldent get up to the American Club last night, but he hadent been getting around much since the strike.*

170   During the Prince of Wales' tour of the United States in 1924, it was reported widely that Rogers had purchased one of the prince's polo ponies for his own use. Actually, Rogers had bought the pony for Florenz Ziegfeld's daughter, Patricia Burke Ziegfeld.

171   *SEP* (July 24, 1926, p. 130): . . . *remembered me. He would be pretty good size even if he had forgotten me.*

172   *SEP* (July 24, 1926, p. 130): . . . *wedding this year. Now, Prince, if I have betrayed any confidence in relating this little small-table talk, I am sorry. I dident ask to come there and I dident ask you any questions. You wasent on your guard what to say, and I certainly wasent nervous in any way. For, to be honest, the whole thing, including the place, seemed to be very ordinary to me. When you talked about anything, you did it as though you were really interested and not doing it for any effect.*

173   *SEP:* Omitted *Special Cable,* May 20, 1926, which appeared in *NYT* datelined August 27, 1926.

174   *SEP:* Omitted letters, May 21 and May 25, 1926.

175   Bernard Mannes Baruch (1870-1965). Successful American businessman who officially advised several presidents and was active in Democratic politics.

176   Pompeii, an ancient Italian city, was buried during a volcanic eruption of nearby Mount Vesuvius (79 A.D.).

177   The *Majestic* was a sister ship of the *Leviathan.* It was originally a German liner known as the *Bismarck,* and was completed at Hamburg by German labor under British supervision in 1921. It was then the largest the world had ever seen and had a tonnage of over 56,000 and a length of 915 feet. It was purchased and operated by the White Star line of Britain.

178   Percival Phillips (1878-1937). Phillips was an American-born member of the British knighthood and correspondent for English newspapers at every warfront from 1907-1937.

179   Margherita Sarfatti (1886-1961). Italian writer and art critic; author of a biography of Mussolini and works on art and artists.

[180] Warren Delano Robbins (1885-1935). Counselor of American embassy in Rome (1925-1928) and ambassador to El Salvador (1928-1930); held other positions in the diplomatic service of the United States.

[181] Hiram Warren Johnson (1866-1945). Progressive governor of California (1911-1917) and Republican U. S. senator (1917-1945); ran unsuccessfully for the vice-presidency on the Progressive party ticket with Theodore Roosevelt (1912).

[182] William Gibbs McAdoo (1863-1941). McAdoo, a successful railroad executive and President Wilson's son-in-law, served as secretary of treasury (1913-1918) and director-general of the railways (1917-1919). The resourceful politician was a prominent candidate for the Democratic presidential nomination (1920, 1924) and later served as United States senator from California (1933-1939).

[183] Aristide Briand (1862-1932). Prime minister of France (1909-1911; 1913; 1921-1922; 1925-1926; 1929). Briand received the Nobel peace prize in 1926 and with United States Secretary of State Kellogg negotiated antiwar Kellogg-Briand pact (1928).

[184] Salvatore Cortesi (1865-1947). Italian journalist and chief of the Rome bureau of the Associated Press. When he joined the Associated Press, he was required to furnish two character references. He promptly submitted the names of the pope and the Italian king.

[185] With the help of government subsidies, Italian shipbuilders turned out several notable vessels between 1926 and 1927, including the *Roma,* a 32,000-ton luxury steamship. The liner was sunk during World War II.

[186] Dinty Moore's restaurant on West Forty-sixth Street in New York City was famous for its good but expensive food. It was a favorite eating place of Will Rogers, Florenz Ziegfeld, Eddie Cantor and other celebrities.

[187] Giuseppe Volpi (1877-1947). Volpi, a wealthy Italian banker, industrialist and statesman, was a member of his country's delegation to the Paris peace conference (1919) and minister of finance (1925-1929). Volpi contributed heavily to the financial support of Italian fascists.

[188] Benjamin Strong (1872-1928). Senior executive with the Banker's Trust Company of New York and first governor of the federal reserve bank of New York (1914-1928).

[189] Rogers might have referred to Fred A. Seaman who, in 1926, was assistant chief, military division, comptroller general's office. At that time the comptroller general's office was a part of the department of the treasury under Secretary Andrew Mellon.

[190] Lincoln Clark Andrews (1867-1950). Assistant secretary of treasury under Andrew Mellon and enforcer of the Prohibition laws (1925-1927). Andrews, a retired brigadier general and career army officer, was dubbed the "field marshal of dry enforcement."

[191] Boies Penrose (1860-1921). Pennsylvania state representative (1884-1886); state senator (1886-1897); and United States senator (1897-1921). Penrose virtually controlled Pennsylvania's Republican party from 1904 until his death.

[197] The Locarno Pact of October 1925 between several European nations (France, Great Britain, Italy, Poland, Czechoslovakia, Belgium and Germany) guaranteed the international boundaries along the Rhine and the demilitarization of the German bank of that river. Within a year of the signings, British and French forces withdrew from the Ruhr and Rhine valleys. Germany first violated the Locarno Pact in March 1926 when troops were sent into the demilitarized zone of the Rhineland.

[193] A Russo-German treaty was signed at Berlin on April 24, 1926. It continued and broadened an earlier agreement (1922) for each state to remain neutral if the other were attacked by a third party, and both were to refuse to take part in any economic boycott of the other. They also promised to maintain warm political and economic ties.

[194] Following World War I, a number of issues arose between Italy and the newly created republic of Yugoslavia, particularly regarding common borders. In the early 1920s the two nations signed a series of agreements in efforts to settle their differences.

[195] In the spring of 1926, Mussolini lent Greek dictator Theodoros Pangalos several million dollars to buy Italian armaments and provisions.

[196] Achille Ambrogio Damiano Ratti (1857-1939). Pope Pius XI (1922-

1939) who signed the Lateran Treaty (1929) with Mussolini by which Vatican City was established and arrangement was made for Italian governmental recognition of the Roman Catholic religion. In 1929 Pope Pius XI described Mussolini as "the man sent to us by Providence."

197   Victor Emmanuel III (1869-1947). King of Italy (1900-1946). With rise of fascism (1922), the king saw his authority decline but chose not to oppose Mussolini for fear of losing his throne. He abdicated (1946) and went into exile in Portugal.

198   Louis "Bull" Montana (1888-1950). Professional wrestler but best remembered as a fierce-faced character actor in early motion pictures.

199   George Herman "Babe" Ruth (1895-1948). Popular baseball star who was playing for the New York Yankees in 1926. He was voted the American League's most valuable player in 1923, and established the career home run mark of 714 which stood until Henry Aaron broke the record in 1974.

200   Robert Marion La Follette (1855-1925). American statesman and political leader who successfully crusaded for reforms and innovations in his home state of Wisconsin. He was a leader of the progressive element of the Republican party. U. S. representative (1885-1891); governor of Wisconsin (1901-1906); U. S. senator (1906-1925). At his death he was replaced in the senate by his son, Robert Marion La Follette, Jr. (1895-1953).

Samuel Gompers (1850-1924). Pioneer American union leader who founded the American Federation of Labor (1886) and served as its president (1886-1894; 1896-1924).

James Joseph "Gene" Tunney (1898-   ). Boxer who in 1926 defeated Jack Dempsey for heavyweight championship (September 23). He retained his title by defeating Dempsey again in 1927, and retired from the ring undefeated a year later.

SEP (July 31, 1926, p. 84): . . . good; Valentino at his peak, the elder Lafolette, a touch of Borah, Bryan of '96, Samuel Gomperts and Jim Furgeson.

201   James M. Munyon (1848-1918). Famous manufacturer and promoter of patent medicines who was fond of saying that he had started with nothing but ambition and a belief in advertising. His famous gesture, with the index finger pointed upward far above his head, and the phrase "there is hope," became familiar through newspaper advertising in many parts of the world.

202   Karl Baedeker (1801-1859). German publisher of traveler's guidebooks. Baedeker issued a guidebook to Coblenz in 1829, and followed it with a series of world famous travel handbooks in German, French and English for most European countries, parts of North America and the Orient. Baedeker's descendants have continued to publish travel guidebooks.

203   Guiseppe Garibaldi (1807-1882). Italian patriot who aided in the unification of Italy.

204   D(avid) W(ark) Griffith (1875-1948). Motion picture producer and director whose most famous film was the Birth of a Nation. In 1919 he formed United Artists Corporation with Mary Pickford, Douglas Fairbanks and Charlie Chaplin. Griffith developed many basic techniques of cinematic art.

205   Birth of a Nation (1915). Produced and directed by D. W. Griffith; first twelve reel motion picture; highly acclaimed Civil War and Reconstruction film which was noted for the introduction of many new movie techniques.

206   The Four Horsemen of the Apocalypse. In 1921 Rex Ingram directed this spectacular version of Ibanez' novel about love, war and death, notable for introducing Rudolph Valentino as an actor.

207   Herbert Johnson (1878-1946). Political cartoonist for the Saturday Evening Post (from 1912). Johnson illustrated the "Letters of a Self-Made Diplomat" series for the Post.

208   Scipione Cardinal Borghese built the Borghese Villa near Rome in 1605. The elaborate edifice is a repository for many of the priceless pieces of art of the Borghese family and the Italian government.

The Louvre is the foremost French museum of art, located in Paris. The original building dates from the reign of Phillip II in the late twelfth century. Phillip's successors added to the building's magnificence and collections, including the Mona Lisa, Venus of Milo and others.

The Smithsonian Institution in Washington, D. C. was founded (1846) under the terms of the will of James Smithson, an intellectually enlightened Englishman who admired the United States. The institution began as a single

137

museum, but has evolved into a vast complex of galleries, museums, research centers, parks and information exchanges.

The Field Museum of Natural History in Chicago is one of the most acclaimed natural history museums in the world. Marshall Field I, Chicago businessman and philanthropist, founded and endowed the museum in 1893.

209 Albert Spalding (1888-1953). American violinist. Spalding composed two violin concertos, a sonata for violin and piano, a suite for violin and piano, and many violin pieces.

210 *SEP* (August 21, 1926, p. 11): . . . *(NOTE TO POST EDITOR: Wasent that Coolidge's college? If it wasent, put in the right one, for nobody over here knows. Very few know Coolidge.)*

Calvin Coolidge entered Amherst College in Massachusetts in the fall of 1891, and graduated *cum laude* in the spring of 1895.

211 John Garibaldi Sargent (1860-1939). Attorney general of Vermont (1908-1912); attorney general of the United States under Coolidge (1925-1929). During his tenure, the portly, unkempt Sargent vigorously supported enforcement of prohibition.

212 The Arkansas River is a major tributary of the Mississippi River. It rises in central Colorado and flows for 1,450 miles through Kansas, northeastern Oklahoma and central and southeastern Arkansas.

The South Canadian River (Canadian River) is 906 miles long and flows through southern Colorado, northeastern New Mexico, northwestern Texas and central Oklahoma. It enters the Arkansas River near Muskogee in eastern Oklahoma.

The Grand River, 406 miles long, is the lower course of the Neosho River which rises in southeastern Kansas and flows through northeastern Oklahoma before entering the Arkansas near Muskogee in eastern Oklahoma.

The Verdigris River runs approximately 350 miles through Kansas and Oklahoma. It flows through Rogers' ranch and empties into the Arkansas River near Muskogee, Oklahoma.

213 Sing Sing was 'for many years the popularized name of a state prison in Ossining, New York. Construction of the prison began in 1825. A number of well-publicized criminals served terms there, and the prison was the scene of countless escapes and near escapes.

214 Michelangelo Buonarroti (1475-1564). Italian sculptor, painter, architect and poet of the high renaissance who decorated the ceilings of the Sistine Chapel (1508-1512), succeeded Sangallo as architect of Saint Peter's Basilica, Rome (1547), and created other enduring works of art.

215 Stanford White (1853-1906). Architect who was member of the firm of McKim, Mead & White, the most important architectural group in the United States until the later twentieth century. Among the buildings designed by White was the old Madison Square Garden, but his most famous structure was the Washington Arch in New York City. White was murdered on the roof of Madison Square Garden.

216 Charles Marion Russell (1865-1926). Famous painter of western scenes and known as the "cowboy artist." Russell was a close friend of Will Rogers. After Russell's death in 1926, his wife published a book of letters he had written to friends, *Good Medicine,* for which Will Rogers wrote the introduction.

217 Elbert Henry Gary (1853-1927). Co-founder of the United States Steel Corporation and chairman of its executive committee (1901-1903); chairman of the board of directors (1903-1927).

John Davison Rockefeller (1839-1937). American oil magnate who organized Standard Oil Company (1870) and became its president.

John Davison Rockefeller, Jr. (1874-1960). Became associated with his father's business interests (1897), and later involved in the philanthropic corporations established by his father.

218 Harry Conway "Bud" Fischer (1884-1954). Cartoonist who created "Mutt and Jeff" comic strip in 1907. Fischer also worked in vaudeville.

Reuben Lucius "Rube" Goldberg (1883-1970). American cartoonist who created the comic strips "Boob McNutt" and "LaLa Palooza." Won a Pultizer prize in 1948. Creator of numerous absurd inventions.

219 Ben Ali Haggin (1882-1951). American portrait painter and socialite who for years was in great demand as an impresario of balls and pageants. Haggin used the Ziegfeld beauties in a tableau effect to recreate famous paintings and

states for the sets of the *Follies*.

220 Raphael (Raffaello Santi) (1483-1520). Italian renaissance painter and chief architect of Saint Peter's Bascilica (1514).

220 Raphael (Raffaello Santi) (1483-1520). Italian renaissance painter and chief architect of Saint Peter's Bascilica (1514).

221 Mammoth Cave is located in southwest central Kentucky and is one of the largest underground caverns in the United States. The cave was first discovered about 1799; the total length of its chambers and passages is about 150 miles. Designated a national park on May 25, 1926.

222 Adolph Simon Ochs (1858-1935). American newspaper publisher; proprietor and publisher, Chattanooga (Tennessee) *Times* (1878-1935); publisher, *New York Times* (1896-1935). Ochs gained control of the declining *New York Times* in 1896 and rebuilt it into one of the world's leading newspapers.

223 *SEP* (August 28, 1926, p. 16): . . . *enthusiastic about relating it.*

I saw Andy Mellon's daughter and Bruce. I never thought Andy would give his daughter's hand in marriage to the son of an avowed wet. And what made it worse was being the son of a Democrat. I couldent believe it when I read it; I thought it was just another bit of propgander for the wets.

The papers over here . . .

224 On May 21, 1926, President Coolidge issued an executive order allowing state, county and municipal officers to receive federal appointments to enforce the dry laws. Prohibition Enforcer Lincoln Andrews campaigned for such powers, which were opposed by a majority of the senate.

225 Dudley Field Malone (1882-1950). Liberal New York defense attorney who was associated with Clarence Darrow in evolution trial in Tennessee (Scopes' trial) which was prosecuted by William Jennings Bryan.

Clarence Seward Darrow (1857-1938). American labor and civil-libertarian attorney who defended Eugene V. Debs in an injunction case arising from the Pullman strike (1895) and John T. Scopes on charges of teaching evolution in the public schools of Tennessee (1925) and was involved in other celebrated cases.

226 Senator William Borah, a highly influential and respected national political figure, delivered a speech at a meeting of the Presbyterian General Assembly in Baltimore (May 30, 1926) assailing the government of New York State for refusing to aid in the enforcement of the Volstead Act. With this and other speeches in support of prohibition, Borah placed himself at the head of the dry movement politically and became one of the most publicized men in the United States.

227 *SEP* (August 28, 1926, p. 16): . . . *you got to make it plain. They make out home in Oklahoma a rabbit and a cayote drive and they are beating the bushes, and everyone . . .*

228 One of the oldest and most famous skyscrapers in New York is the Flatiron Building, located on Twenty-third Street where Broadway crosses Fifth Avenue. The twenty-one-story building was completed in 1903; it has a triangular shape like that of an old-fashioned flatiron.

229 Herbert Clark Hoover (1874-1964). United States president (1929-1933); mining engineer; U. S. food administrator during World War I; established American relief administration; secretary of commerce under both Harding and Coolidge (1921-1928).

230 Frank Orren Lowden (1861-1943). American lawyer and politician; Republican U. S. representative (1906-1911); governor of Illinois (1917-1921). In 1920 Lowden was a leading candidate for the presidential nomination but his connection with industrialist George Pullman (he had married Pullman's elder daughter in 1896) and high style of living militated against his gaining the support of many laborers and small farmers.

231 Edouard Herriot (1872-1957). French statesman and political leader who served as premier (1924-1925; 1932) and held other major offices in the French government after World War I.

232 Raymond Poincare (1860-1934). Conservative French statesman, writer and politician during 1910s and 1920s. Poincare served intermittently as premier (1912-1913; 1922-1924; 1926-1929), and as finance minister (1926-1929) caused measures to be passed that stablized the franc.

233 Mohammed Abd-el-Krim el Khattabi (1881-1963). Leader of Moors in disputed Riff region of Morocco who was successful in his war with the Spanish (1921-1924). In 1925 he attacked the French zone but was defeated by a combined French and Spanish force (1926) and exiled. The "Wolf of the

Riff" became a legend and established a worldwide reputation in his desert wars against the French and Spanish in Morocco.

234 *SEP:* Omitted the *Special Cable,* June 24, which appeared in *NYT,* September 19, 1926.

235 *NYT* (September 19, 1926, II:1): . . . *at first expected.*

P.S.—Have stood all day at the airdrome looking for Fonck. If he don't start tomorrow, send Ederle and Corson.

Yours for Parisian news and fashions.

WILL ROGERS.

236 Myron Timothy Herrick (1854-1929). American political leader and diplomat. Republican governor of Ohio (1903-1905); United States ambassador to France (1912-1914; 1921-1929).

237 Victor-Henri Berenger (1867-1952). The French ambassador to the United States (1925-1926) who signed the war debt settlement between the United States and France known as the Mellon-Berenger accord (1926). The arrangements proved to be far from final, and the bulk of the debts was never paid.

238 Harry Lauder (1870-1950). Scottish singer who gained popularity for his Scottish songs, many of his own composition. Sir Harry was one of the most popular entertainers of history. There were so many reports of his retirement that he jokingly referred to one of his forty-five trips to the United States as his "seventh farewell tour."

239 Marcus Alonzo "Mark" Hanna (1837-1904). American businessman and politician who supported William McKinley for president and served as chairman of the Republican national committee, raising from large business a campaign fund of unprecedented size. Hanna served as United States senator from Ohio (1897-1904), as well as being McKinley's closest adviser.

240 *SEP:* Omitted the *Special Cable,* June 26, which appeared in *NYT,* August 27, 1926, datelined London, August 26, 1926.

241 *SEP* (August 28, 1926, p. 123): . . . *his own relief.*

I had just come from down in Italy and had a siege with this Party Mussolini, him being the biggest headliner in Europe today. Well, I found . . .

242 Miguel Primo de Rivera y Orbaneja (1870-1930). Spanish general and dictator who ascended to power after a bloodless revolution (1923). Primo de Rivera was initially supported by the Spanish king and army officers but finally forced by them to retire (1930). He died suddenly in Paris.

243 Ogden Haggerty Hammond (1869-1956). Republican businessman and politician from New Jersey; American ambassador to Spain (1925-1929).

244 Alexander Pollock Moore (1867-1930). Colorful editor, diplomat and native of Pittsburgh. Moore was editor-in-chief of the Pittsburgh *Leader* (from 1904). He also served as American ambassador to Spain (1923-1925), Peru (1928-1930) and Poland (1930).

245 Charles Henry Cunningham (1885-1945?). Government career officer; commercial attaché, U. S. department of commerce, Spain (1920-1923), Portugal (1921-1923), Cuba (1923-1924), Spain and Portugal (1924-1927), Peru and Equador (1929-1931) and Mexico City (1931-1933).

246 Vicente Blasco-Ibáñez (1867-1928). Spanish novelist, ardent republican and revolutionary politician. Two of his best works were *La Barraca* and *Canas y barro,* but his most popular novel was *Los Cuatro jinetes del apocalipsis (The Four Horsemen of the Apocalypse).*

247 Spain and Brazil were charter members of the League of Nations, an international organization founded after World War I and dedicated to peace. Germany applied for membership to the League and was accepted as a permanent member of the organization's General Council (1926). In the reshuffling of the limited number of permanent seats, the League reassigned Spain and Brazil non-permanent status. The realignment generated considerable controversy and, eventually, both Spain and Brazil withdrew from the League.

248 *SEP* (August 28, 1926, p. 125): . . . *disarming with you too. But the way they are setting, every one of them over here with fortified borders all around them, I wouldent only not disarm but I would go get another gun.*

I know one Nation over here if I dident have any more friends around me than she has, I not only would sleep with a Pistol in each hand but if I was them I wouldent go to sleep at all. I would just set up and watch. There is a lot . . .

249 W. Freeland Kendrick (1874-1953). Mayor of Philadelphia (1924-1928); past imperial potentate of shriners; originator of idea of shriners' hospital for crippled children, now operating in various cities.

250 Smedley Darlington Butler (1881-1940). Major General Butler of the United States marine corps took a leave of absence to act as director of the department of safety of Philadelphia (1924-1925). Hardnosed, Butler was appointed to enforce prohibition in crime-ridden Philadelphia. After one year the number of arrests for liquor violations rose from 1,413 to 6,080, but the rate of convictions was less than four percent. After two years Butler had become such a nuisance to Philadelphia that Coolidge acceded to public pressure and orderd him back to the marines.

251 Cornelius "Connie Mack" McGillicuddy (1862-1956). Baseball catcher who became owner and manager of the Philadelphia Athletics of the American League in 1901 and managed until 1950.

Arthur "Artie" Fletcher (1885-1950). Shortstop for the New York Giants (1909-1920). Fletcher played briefly for the Philadelphia Phillies of the National League (1920-1922) and then managed the team (1923-1926), but had two cellar squads and never got the club higher than sixth place. He later coached the New York Yankees of the American League (1927-1945).

252 It is not certain to whom Rogers was referring.

253 Mariano Montes (1894-1926). Spanish matador killed near Madrid in the Plaza Vista Alegre by the bull Gallego.

254 Jacobo Fitz-James Stuart y Falcó (1878-1953). Seventeenth Duke of Alba and descendant of James II of England; possessed the largest collection of titles held by a European noble. When his father died in 1902, he inherited more than thirty-three titles, estates throughout Spain, a castle in almost every important city in that country and a collection of art that led the Duke in time to become one of the world's leading authorities on the subject.

255 *SEP:* Omitted this and succeeding *Special Cables;* they appeared in the *New York Times* as "daily telegrams."

256 Secretary of the Treasury Andrew Mellon traveled through Europe from July-September 1926 to discuss war debts with foreign leaders.

257 Suzanne Lenglen (1899-1938). French lawn-tennis player who won world's hardcourt (women's) singles championship at Paris (1913) and won championships in singles, doubles and mixed doubles of France and England (1919-1923; 1925-1926). She turned professional (1926) at the urging of C. C. Pyle, sports promoter, but retired after one year touring the United States.

258 C(harles) C. Pyle (1881-1939). One of America's most colorful sports promoters who persuaded Harold "Red" Grange to turn professional and later managed Grange for several years. Pyle was credited with having caused Suzanne Lenglen, Mary Browne, Vincent Richards and other tennis stars to desert the amateur ranks.

259 George Bernard Shaw (1856-1950). British playwright, novelist and critic. By 1926 he was established as the leading British playwright of his time; awarded Nobel prize for literature (1925).

260 During July, August and September 1926, twenty-two swimmers, including eight women, attempted to swim the channel.

261 *NYT* (August 5, 1926, p. 23): . . . *says we borrowed the money, but we doubt it.*

262 General Andrews, tough prohibition enforcer, conferred with British officials in an effort to stem the flow of smuggled British liquor into the United States. Despite the arrangements made at this meeting, the tide of contraband liquor was never curtailed effectively.

263 *NYT* (August 8, 1926, p. 1, section 2): . . . *Aug. 7.—Mr. Coolidge has just sent Mr. Mellon over to Italy . . .*

264 Gertrude Caroline "Trudy" Ederle (1906-   ). American swimming champion who was the first woman to swim the English Channel. On August 6, 1926, Trudy Ederle swam the channel from Cape Grisnez, France, to Kingsdown, England, completing the thirty-five miles in a record setting time of fourteen hours and thirty-one minutes.

265 Georges Eugene Benjamin Clemenceau (1841-1929). Premier of the third French republic (1906-1909; 1917-1920). In August 1926 Clemenceau wrote an open letter to President Coolidge admitting France was a debtor nation, but would remain totally independent.

141

266 American tourists were flooding Europe at this time, and were displaying their money in such a way as to provoke European resentment. President Coolidge asked Americans to be considerate and remember they were guests of the other nations.

267 London and many other cities in England reported slight tremors on August 15. Practically no damage was done anywhere by the shocks.

268 A championship cricket series between Australian and British teams had begun June 12, 1926, and had produced no decision through four matches. The fifth and deciding match began August 15, 1926, and was held on the Kensington Oval in London. Britain was the eventual winner.

269 George Frederick Ernest Albert (1865-1936). King George V; succeeded to the English throne in 1910. He was not in Scotland when Rogers and the newspapers believed he was, but was grouse hunting.

270 Rogers referred to Secretary of State Kellogg's speech of August 18 in Plattsburg, New York, which dedicated the memorial to Thomas Macdonough, early-day American naval commander. In the speech Kellogg spoke of world disarmament.

271 Leading Filipinos were pressuring the United States for complete autonomy; therefore President Coolidge sent a personal representative to the islands to gather information that eventually would lead to Filipino independence.

272 *NYT* (August 22, 1926, I:5):
LONDON, Aug. 21—Germany just keeps on paying her reparations and never saying a word.
You can afford to do that when you have lost a war and don't have any army and navy to support.
Yours for relief of the Oklahoma farmers, particularly,
WILL ROGERS.

273 Theodoros Pangalos (1878-1952). Overthrew Greek president in June 1925; briefly he was dictator, but was removed by an army coup on August 22, 1926. After his overthrow he sought safety out of the country by hiding in a ship's wireless turret. He was caught and taken to Athens.
The hippopotamus was the first born in captivity since 1922.

274 George Michael Cohan (1878-1942). American actor, playwright and producer; author also of many popular songs, including "I'm a Yankee Doodle Dandy," "You're a Grand Old Flag," "Give My Regards to Broadway" and "Over There."

275 Chautauqua was a summer entertainment and educational movement. Many artists and speakers appeared on these cultural programs for small towns.

276 William Thomas Cosgrave (1880-1965). Third president of the Irish Free State (1922-1932), and one of the leading figures of the Irish Revolution.

277 John William Davis (1873-1955). West Virginia lawyer and politician. United States ambassador to Great Britain (1918-1921); Democratic candidate for president in opposition to Coolidge in 1924.

278 Martin Edwin Trapp (1877-1951). Democratic lieutenant governor of Oklahoma (1914; 1919-1923); succeeded to the office of governor (November 19, 1923) when John C. Walton was removed following his impeachment and conviction; served as governor from 1923-1927.

279 *NYT* (September 10, 1926, p. 23): *DUBLIN, Sept. 9.*

280 *NYT* (August 2, 1926, p. 19): *LONDON, Aug. 1.*

281 Tammany Hall. Name applied to Democratic party organization in New York City.

282 *SEP* (October 2, 1926, p. 6):
Dear Mr. Coolidge: My job is, of course, to find out all I can and report to you. The reason I have not reported lately is because I havent found out anything much lately, and I am not like a lot of people to bother you when I really have nothing to take up with you but your time.
Well, I have . . .

283 *SEP* (October 2, 1926, p. 170): . . . *each other. Nobody wanted disarmament.*

284 *SEP* (October 2, 1926, p. 170): . . . *you never hear anybody speak of, yet it is a greater boost for more wars than anything—that is the . . .*

285 *SEP* (October 2, 1926, p. 170): . . . *debts. We can cancel all the debts in the world and they will say, "Well, we shamed you into it."*

286 Arica is a seaport city in the Tarapaca province of extreme northern

142

Chile; Tacna is a region in extreme southern Peru. Tacna-Arica was the center of a dispute which long embittered Chilean-Peruvian relations and finally erupted in hostilities (1921-1929). In June 1926 United States mediators interceded but failed to end the dispute through a plebiscite. In 1930 the region was divided between the two South American nations; Peru received Tacna and Chile secured Arica.

[287] *SEP* (October 2, 1926, p. 173): *. . . you answer his.*

Borah has had an answer for everything over there, but nobody has had an answer for Borah over here. I may drop . . .

[288] Thaddeus Horatius Caraway (1871-1931). Democratic U. S. representative from Arkansas (1913-1921); U. S. senator (1921-1931). Caraway co-authored the McNary-Haugen farm relief bill; he sharply criticized Coolidge for vetoing it.

Byron Patton "Pat" Harrison (1881-1941). Democratic U. S. representative from Mississippi (1911-1919); U. S. senator (1919-1941).

James Middleton Cox (1870-1957). Journalist and political leader from Ohio. U. S. representative (1909-1913); governor (1913-1915; 1917-1921); Democratic candidate for president in 1920, but lost to Warren G. Harding in a Republican landslide.

[289] Dorothy Gish (1898-1968). American actress and sister of actress Lillian Gish. First appeared on the stage at age four and subsequently performed in other plays, movies and television. While in London in 1926, Miss Gish filmed *Tiptoes* with Will Rogers and Nelson Keys for British National Film Company.

Nora Bayes (Dora Goldberg) (1880-1928). American actress; widely known in vaudeville and musical comedy; performed often with Will Rogers.

[290] *SEP* (October 2, 1926, p. 173): *. . . visiting England now.*

I see where Ambassador of France Herrick come over. That was just as well. He had made speeches to about everybody over here, so there was practically nothing left to do. Poincare will soon . . .

[291] *SEP* (October 2, 1926, p. 173): *. . . stop, as I have to stand on my head this afternoon to kiss the Blarney Stone.*

[292] *NYT* (August 28, 1926, p. 13):

LONDON, Aug. 27—American tourists are still coming by the thousands and bragging about where they come from. Sometimes you think France really has been too lenient with them.

Yours for quieter visitors.

WILL ROGERS.

NYT (August 29, 1926, I:3):

LONDON, Aug. 28.—Another American woman just now swam in from France. Her husband was carried from the boat suffering from cold and exposure. She has two children, the smallest a girl, who is swimming over tomorrow.

Yours for a revised edition of the Dictionary explaining which is the weaker sex.

WILL ROGERS.

NYT (August 30, 1926, p. 3):

LONDON, Aug. 29.—A man came within thirty yards of swimming the Thames River here today. He was dragged out when overcome. It's the nearest any man has come to swimming the river since 1889.

Immigration authorities are barring any woman that comes from America if she is found to have a bathing suit. Is there any way I can change my sex? I am becoming humiliated.

Yours weakly.

WILL ROGERS.

[293] A labor party member had interrupted debate in the House of Commons during late August and was suspended from the "service of the House." A similar outburst had occurred in Washington during the last session of Congress.

[294] Newton Diehl Baker (1871-1937). Lawyer and United States secretary of war (1916-1921). On August 29, 1926, Baker called for mutual cancellation of all war debts.

[295] John Berry Hobbs (1882-1963). He was the hero of the test matches with Australia (see footnote 268); generally regarded as the greatest batsman in cricket; knighted by Queen Elizabeth II (1953).

[296] On August 29, 1926, Mrs. Clemington Corson of New York swam the English Channel from Cape Grisnez, France, to Dover, England in fifteen

hours and twenty-eight minutes. Mrs. Corson, a mother of two children, was only the second woman and seventh individual to accomplish the feat. On the following day Ernst Vierkoetter of Germany swam nearly the same route and set a record of twelve hours and forty-three minutes. Vierkoetter rested on an English beach for twenty minutes following his swim and then immediately returned by tug to France.

297 Charles Evans Hughes (1862-1948). American jurist and politician. Governor of New York (1907-1910); unsuccessful Republican presidential candidate, defeated by Wilson (1916); secretary of state (1921-1925); chief justice, United States Supreme Court (1930-1941).

298 *NYT* (September 3, 1926, p. 19):
LONDON, Sept. 2.—Say, what is all this argument about who is to fly over here and who ain't? If they don't hurry up some American woman of European nationality will swim the thing. What difference does it make? Somebody will break their record the next week anyway. Throw 'em all out and send Colonel Mitchell.
Yours for congenial aviation.

WILL ROGERS.

299 The United States was inaugurating a five year naval aviation expansion program, and Rogers referred to President Coolidge's executive statement assuring other countries that the United States was not violating the Washington arms treaty.

300 *NYT* (September 6, 1926, p. 17): . . . *disarm.*
Them game fish up there in that lake has giv Cal some new backbone.
Yours . . .

301 Harry Kendall Thaw (1871-1947), Evelyn Nesbit (1884-1967). He was known as a wealthy playboy. She was an artist's model, dancer and actress. In 1906 Thaw killed one of her former suitors, Stanford White, prominent New York architect (see footnote 215). He was institutionalized as criminally insane until 1915. Thaw and Nesbit were divorced in 1916, but rumors prevailed in 1926 that they were reconciling.

302 *NYT* (September 7, 1926, p. 23):
P. S.—I know you all read of the terrible movie disaster in Ireland yesterday. Well, I am going to Dublin on Wednesday to give a benefit for them. Cable over what you can, either to me at the Hotel Shelbourne or to President Cosgrave. It's a real cause. Thanks.

303 *NYT* (September 12, 1926, I:13):
BERLIN, Sept. 11.—I flew here from Dublin—looked over the edge of the plane and saw a Frenchman breaking the record swimming the English Channel.
Arrived in Berlin this afternoon in time to see Dr. Peltzer beat Nurmi and his record.
Will arrive home in November, 1928, and see just how fast Cal is.

Yours,
WILL ROGERS.

304 *NYT* (September 13, 1926, p. 23): *BERLIN,* . . .

305 Rogers had seen Dr. Otto Peltzer (1900-1970), a German school teacher, run a 1500-meter race against Edvin Wide, a Swedish athlete, and against the famed Finnish runner Paavo Nurmi (1897-1973). Peltzer beat Wide and Nurmi by less than three meters. Wide defeated Nurmi in the two-mile run the next afternoon, but Nurmi regained the two-mile record in 1931.

306 *NYT* (September 18, 1926 p. 19): . . . *see the castles.*
Just flew in here this afternoon from Cologne. If Fonck don't hurry up and start, I will fly over from this end. We will fly that far over here every day.
Yours for timely and accurate news anywhere but in the Alps.

WILL ROGERS.

307 *NYT* (September 20, 1926, p. 25):
PARIS, Sept. 19.—We are still setting here, looking up, waiting for that Frenchman to come by air.
These Frenchmen over here are advising him to jump if he don't get any further than Sandy Hook.
They can stand him lighting in the water, but they can't stand this delay.
Yours for a man that don't stand with his knees bent so long.

WILL ROGERS.

308 *NYT* (September 21, 1926, p. 31): . . . *is getting beat.*

We all used to tell a lot of jokes about Florida, mostly because we were jealous of her wonderful possibilities, and then we knew she was able to stand it, but now that she is in real trouble, she will find everybody has always loved her and admired her at heart.

What's the matter with Al Smith's plans? He is as long making up his mind to jump as Rene Fonck is. Being Governor of even New York beats nothing until a little later on when something better might show up.

Don't run for that Senate. You would be sunk in there. They wouldn't listen to Abraham Lincoln his first ten years in there if he was to come back and be elected to it.

Yours,
WILL ROGERS.

[309] *NYT* (September 25, 1926, p. 8):

ABOARD THE S. S. LEVIATHAN, Sept. 25.—With ex-Secretary Hughes to work with, raised $30,000 tonight for Florida.

We will have their clothes before we land.

WILL ROGERS.

P. S.—Glad to hear Kearns won the big fight.

[310] The United States Shipping Board, the *Leviathan's* operators, arranged for Will Rogers, former Secretary of State Charles Evans Hughes and actor-author James Gleason to perform to all three classes of the ship's passengers thereby raising money for the victims of a devastating hurricane in Florida. The group raised $40,600, one of the largest sums ever raised on an ocean liner.

[311] Milton Snavely Hershey (1857-1945). Millionaire chocolate manufacturer and noted philanthropist. Gave $8,000 to see Rogers repeat the act.

INDEX

148